The *Professional* Amenity Plant

Appraisal Handbook

The *Professional* Amenity Plant

Appraisal Handbook

Marty Shaw, RCA

Acclaim Press
Your Next Great Book

P.O. Box 238
Morley, MO 63767
(573) 472-9800
www.acclaimpress.com

Cover & Book Design: M. Frene Melton

ISBN: 978-1-942613-91-6 | 1-942613-91-1
Library of Congress Control Number: 2018901807

First Printing: 2018
Printed in the United States of America
10 9 8 7 6 5 4 3 2 1

Contents

Dedication

This book is dedicated to all of those who have striven to understand, qualify, quantify and simplify the practice of professional amenity plant appraisal. Without your dedication and hard work, this book would not have been possible. It is my sincere hope that this book will take some of the mystery out of the practice of professional amenity plant appraisal and provide fertile ground for a deeper understanding and future refinement of our craft.

To quote my friend and mentor Joe McNeil, "Professional amenity plant appraisal is not easy, and it is not simple." When I first embarked on this journey over 20 years ago, I was young, naïve and foolish enough to think that this stuff was simple and easy. I thought that right up to the point when I took on my first appraisal assignment and I had to do it for real. The reality set in and I had no other arborists around to guide me down the path to forming a reliable and credible opinion. Even though I had the eighth edition of the CTLA guide, there were vast gaps in what I needed to know, leaving me to fill the gaps the best I could. Much of what I thought I knew in the beginning was simply wrong. Most of what I thought I knew was completely out of step with other forms of appraisal practice, especially the practice of professional real estate appraisal. Since those early days, I have worked with dozens of real estate appraisers and I have attained the prerequisite education and training of a real estate appraiser instructor, a real estate broker instructor, I attained the ASCA RCA designation and I became a BCMA.

As a real estate appraiser instructor, I have had a chance to reorganize my thinking about plants and plant appraisal and I have had ample opportunity to research and study this subject matter in depth. I have also had long discussions over the years with other professional amenity plant appraisers who, like me, have had years of experience, education and training on the subject. The hours of review and feedback that I have received from the likes of Lew Bloch, Joe Samnik, Russ Carlson, Scott Cullen, Tom Smiley, David Hucker, Julian Dunster and many others have sharpened my thinking and helped me to organize my thoughts more clearly and concisely.

Preface

The practice of professional **amenity**[1] plant **appraisal** (**PAL**) has gained wide acceptance as a specialized area of professional **specialty appraisal practice**. The purpose of this book is to provide **arborists**, green industry professionals, insurance people, accountants, real **estate** appraisal specialists, attorneys or others involved in related professions with an objective and independent resource that briefly explains the history, the underlying principles and the various methodologies that are well-rooted in sound appraisal theory and that have been refined over the years. Plant appraisal has enjoyed growing **credibility** for over a hundred years now, and this long-trusted tradition continues to be an important area in specialty appraisal practice. The effort of this book continues that tradition by carrying forward even more refinements in plant appraisal and offers greater clarity to the practice of amenity plant appraisal — especially to newcomers who are just starting out as appraisal specialists. It is also a great resource for veteran plant appraisers or for those who are just curious to know more.

Another purpose of this book is to build upon the bridge of previously published work in professional plant appraisal, both in tomes and peer-reviewed work, to provide professional plant appraisers (PAs) with a deeper understanding and to reach further insights into the **relevance**, **reliability** and credibility of PAL work. The principles and procedures described in this book are currently practiced in appraising the value of amenity **landscape** shade and ornamental (**ALSO**) trees. As the work of professional amenity plant appraisers (PAs) becomes even more widely known as an appraisal specialty, the need for ALSO plant appraisals will likewise continue to grow.

The outline of this book is as straightforward a reference as you will find. It begins with a brief history of the need for professional plant appraisal and briefly describes those needs. The basic underlying principles of value and appraisal work are discussed, and the overall appraisal process is described. I then discuss the various elements that must be identified in the appraisal

[1] Words appearing in **bold** are included in the Glossary.

problem to be solved and the scope of work that encompasses the amenity plant appraisal problem solving activity. The next and largest part of this book takes a detailed look at the most common characteristics of plants and sites that may be relevant to solving a wide range of PAL problems. That is, we take a careful look at plant/**site analysis** of how plants can provide anticipated benefits and we examine how those anticipated benefits can be perceived as valuable in utility. We also take a careful look at the physical ability of plants to deliver on those benefits and we look at how deficiencies in the delivery of benefits can adversely affect amenity plant values. We then take a careful look at the various appraisal approaches, methods of analysis and processes that are used in the calculation of ethical, credible and reliable opinions of value for amenity landscape shade and ornamental (ALSO) plants. Finally, we take a brief look at the various ways in which appraisal opinions are communicated to clients for the varied uses of professional amenity plant appraisals (PALs).

As a matter of practicality, the relevant plant **species** adaptability characteristics are found in the Site Characteristics section, but site and species characteristics are relative to one another. To assist newcomers to the practice of plant appraisal, I have also included a short primer on **landscape architectural design**. Understanding how plants fit into the landscape architectural **design criteria** is a vital skill that is needed in understanding the value of benefits that landscape plants deliver. The critical and unique skills that an ALSO plant appraiser must possess include: the ability to objectively identify the ALSO plant benefits, the ability to analyze a plant's ability to deliver ALSO benefits, the ability to identify any deficiencies in the plant's ability to deliver ALSO benefits and the ability to calculate deficiency in terms of relative importance in the amenity plant appraisal process. While no single resource could possibly equip a PA to do all that PAL entails, this book will provide a comprehensive framework upon which to build. For those who want to take the credible and reliable craft of PAL out of the realm of mystery and into the realm of quantifiable dollars and cents, this is the book for you. If you simply want to know why it is that landscape trees and shrubs are loved so dearly by so many, this book goes a long way to answering that question.

DISCLAIMER: The author of this book is not an attorney and does not practice law. Nothing in this book is to be considered as legal advice or law practice. Any questions about legal matters should be discussed with an attorney. While some issues of governmental force are discussed in this book, those discussions are only provided to serve as aids to understanding certain nuances in the specialty appraisal practice of PAL.

The *Professional* Amenity Plant

Appraisal Handbook

CHAPTER ONE

BACKGROUND

EVER SINCE THE ENGLISH FEUDAL SYSTEM STARTED TO GIVE way to private land ownership rights in the Middle Ages, beginning circa 1290, neighbors have valued their property rights with great anticipation. As one of the earliest commentators, William Blackstone, understood it, property rights are "that sole and despotic dominion which one man claims over the external things of the world, in total exclusion of the right of any other individual in the universe." It is this undergirding privilege and right of ownership that lured seven million Americans, 40 percent of the nation's population, to follow in the steps of Daniel Boone and move west over the Appalachian Mountains by 1840. The 1803 Louisiana Purchase made it possible for Americans to own prime farm land at little or no cost and this new, American, pioneering spirit eagerly abandoned the eastward European life and livelihood and (at great risk and great personal industry) settled the new territory that lay ahead of them. The new American spirit was born.

At that time, the primary use of land was farming. Trees were used as fuel and were a must because of the many things you can make from their wood fiber. In pioneering days, land that contained no trees was considered to be worthless, grassy desert. Since then, of course, property values have improved and, to accommodate this prosperity, society has grown to become far more interdependent. Now, many laws, regulations and ordinances have been put in place (by both the courts and legislatures at all levels) to assist private landowners and governments in orderly and equitable conduct regarding land and its uses. (Nolon, 2017)

The use of trees has expanded well beyond the necessity of timber or fuel and now includes a broad range of functional and aesthetic amenity benefits. In fact, Americans spend billions of dollars each year in the pursuit of improving their land in the attainment of those very amenity tree benefits. As more and more people rely on knowledgeable tree experts and counselors, neighbors will invariably become better educated and more knowledgeable about the legalities that trees present and the need for PAs is continually expanding.

The need for plant appraisal has existed since the early part of the twentieth century. As reported by Cullen, tree and plant valuation methods are simply tools. They cannot be used meaningfully without a fundamental understanding of how the basic concepts came into being and how appraisal results are used to fulfill a need. This includes any form of opinion about amenity plant value and valuation. The framework of contemporary plant appraisal practice and procedures began to take shape more than a century ago.

In the early days of plant appraisal, individuals developed or compiled methods of appraising the value of trees for various purposes. The lack of continuity among plant appraisers and appraisals lead to wildly divergent opinions of tree value across the land. The problem created credibility gaps for decision-makers everywhere and the credibility gap still persists, albeit in somewhat diminished fashion, to this day. In 1947, the 23rd National Shade Tree Conference recognized the need to form a consensus, so they initiated a committee to devise an agreed-upon amenity tree valuation method. In 1951, the committee's work was presented and by 1957, the first industry guidance on tree value was published by the National Arborist Association (now the Tree Care Industry Association).

Since then, various organizations have joined the effort to improve the processes and procedures that PAs use in their tree valuation efforts and these same processes and procedures have been refined with new, additional methods to fill an ever-broadening range of specific plant appraisal needs. Each progressive development in the understanding and refinement of PAL has been accompanied by improved guidance and clarity.

In 1975, a revision of the guidance expanded to include both trees and other plants and the advent of The **Council of Tree and Landscape Appraisers** (CTLA), which brought together a consortium of green industry organization representatives to create a broader consensus body. CTLA has effectively brought accord among the various branches of the green industry by offering nine published editions of guidance between 1957 and 2000; the most recent edition is entitled *Guide for Plant Appraisal, 9th Ed.* (**GPA9**) This guide has been the primary source of guidance to PAs since 2000. In recent years, CTLA has been unable to reach a similar consensus among their respective member organizations and many of the member representatives have changed or individual members have departed due to disagreements over the thrust and direction of future published guidance. This impasse and the lack of competently credentialed subject matter experts being adapted into the current CTLA membership has caused many poorly conceived drafts of the CTLA guide. That has led directly to the need of and effort contained within this book. What is needed is an authoritative, independent and objective voice to clear out the mystery and illuminate the relevant facts when a decision of competent judgment is required about the value of trees and landscaping.

Various Needs Call for Professional Plant Appraisal

Tort damages, insurance coverage, condemnation, arbitration, mediation, real estate transactions, land use and development, municipal management, environmental system service estimates, tax deductions for losses and donations, asset management, resource allocation and many other situations often call for a decision about trees.

Amenity trees are unique among land improvements in that they can possess characteristics that retain both the potential of great worth as an investment that appreciates over time and they can possess the potential for great liability that can also become greater over time. Decision makers need to know how large a tree liability might be or how much a tree is worth. Each plant or tree appraisal assignment brings with it a unique set of facts and circumstance, making the PA's task both complex and challenging. Added to that, the need to know is critically important to those involved in the decision-making process and the question of a plant's value must be answered to the best that it can be answered. Because the PA's opinion is important to appraisal users, it may be scrutinized in the extreme. The reward of being tested, however difficult the challenge, will certainly result in the PA establishing more relevance and credibility, having gained greater clarity in the effort. It is increasingly important for PAs (and others) to perceive the practice of professional plant appraisal as a worthwhile and credible endeavor.

Those who benefit from your work will do so in the light of day rather than in the blind fumbling and stumbling that plagues so many in the darkness of ignorance. That has, too often, been the hallmark of times past. Here now is a partial list of some common contemporary uses of professional plant appraisal adapted from Cullen:

- Amenity valuation (O'Callaghan 2000, Helliwell 2003, Cullen, *et al.* 2006)
- Budget justification and setting (Parker 1915, Armstrong 1947, Felt 1930, Cullen *et al.* 2006, I-TREE.ORG 2006)

- Condemnation — eminent domain (CTLA 2000, Hoy 2002) (United States v Lorance)
- Damage claims (Stone 1916, Pack 1922, Armstrong (generally) 1947, Felt 1930, CTLA 2000, O'Callaghan 2000, Helliwell 2003)
- Insurance (CTLA 2000)
- Subsidence (Cullen *et al.* 2006) (specifically)
- Tax deductions (Armstrong 1947, Felt 1930, CTLA 2000)
- Trespass and vandalism (CTLA 2000, Cullen *et al.* 2006)
- Real estate value contribution (Parker 1915, Stone 1916, CTLA 2000 Tyrväinen and Miettinen 2000)
- Setting fines under §210 of the T&CPA. (O'Callaghan 2000)
- Urban forest management, planning and decision making (Pemberton 1967, CTLA 2000)
- Cost/Benefit analysis in risk assessment

What is value?

To value something is to hold that thing in high esteem or with a high regard. Let's say that thing is a family photograph or a family heirloom of some sort. To the owner of that thing, its value may be priceless (because of its associated emotional or sentimental inspiration) so that no price could be paid to inspire the owner to part with it. To someone else, the same thing may only be of value because of its importance in history with no other sentiment at all. To others, that same thing may be of little or no value at all because the constituent components of which the thing is made are easily obtained and replaced and are not at all unique to the thing itself. To have value, a thing must have scarcity. For example: to the average American, atmospheric oxygen is plentiful and flows freely everywhere. Oxygen (in air) cannot be controlled to any significance and is available to all people all the time in roughly the same amounts. While oxygen is important and critical to life, it is also abundant that there is generally no need to pay money for it. Oxygen does not hold an emotional attachment or specially attract someone's opinion with high regard because it is always there.

However, anyone who has been deprived of oxygen for any period can tell you that oxygen is quite tangible and is neither abstract nor ephemeral and any chemist can tell you that oxygen is not difficult to qualify and quantify. Having served as a member of the crew aboard the USS *Shark* (SSN 591, a submarine), I was keenly aware of the need for oxygen in the air we breathed. In today's submarines, oxygen is generated through simple electrolysis of catalyzed water, splitting it into pure oxygen and hydrogen. The oxygen is released into the air and the hydrogen is pumped overboard. Most commercially available oxygen is produced this way today.

In the old days, before oxygen generators were invented, if our air become low in oxygen and we could not go near the surface to replenish (because of where we were and what we were doing) we replenished the air by burning chlorate candles. A chlorate candle is an oxygen generator that contains a mix of sodium chlorate and iron powder. When ignited, it reacts at 1,112°F, producing sodium chloride, iron oxide and an abundant amount of oxygen. Burning these candles permitted operation of the submarine completely submerged for extended periods of time. We had to use these very messy candles a few times aboard the *Shark* while operating in some hairy environments, but that is another story for another time.

Any gas distributor the world over can tell you that the packaging of elemental oxygen is a straightforward process and that it may be exchanged for the monies that it costs to produce it in any given form. Any patient that requires extra oxygen because of disease can tell you what it means to them to be able to breathe freely. Depending on the unique circumstances of each person, the value of oxygen may vary. There is no right value or wrong value; there is only value to whom or an opinion of value based on the relevant characteristics of the appraisal problem. The value of a thing may only be found in the anticipated enjoyment of benefits that owning a thing entails. (Appraisal Institute, 2010)

The market venue contains both the industry of supply and the desire of demand. It provides the means of exchange in terms of money. In a free and open market venue, the buyers and sellers are compelled to transact only by their willingness to freely engage in an exchange transaction. Of course, not all transaction of property occurs at **arm's length** and there are forces that exist that cause exchange to occur outside of the bounds of a free and open marketplace.

In fact, when it comes to the need for amenity tree appraisals, there are far more instances where an opinion of value is needed that fall outside the confines of the free and open marketplace than there are instances that occur within it, particularly when the question comes to contributory real estate market value (CREMV) in comparative sales of **real estate** transactions. More on that later.

How do you put a price on someone or something you love dearly? What type of exchange could you give to have something like the deep and abiding love and companionship that 50 years of marriage encompasses? These are values that cannot be bought or sold at any price. While some would likewise place similar esoteric value on things like trees and landscaping, those types of value problems bring about serious philosophical questions that can go well beyond the abilities and scope of work the that serious PAs are routinely expected to perform. Plant appraisers are called upon to answer a specific question of money value and to form opinions and conclusions that are supported by facts, evidence and the analysis of reliable, relevant data. Certainly, the courts of jurisdiction may be sympathetic to people's feelings and may be sympathetic about the intangible realities that those feelings conjure, but it is almost always the case that the best the courts can do is provide relief in the form of money in their place and there are judicial mechanisms to affect that relief when it is warranted. Those questions of esoteric value that tend to evoke unfounded judgments based only on a kneejerk reaction are best left to others.

So, the question of value (for the purposes of the PA) will always come down to an opinion of value to whom in exchange for money. The appraisal problem must be boiled down to economics. To prepare an answer and to form a quantifiable opinion about the economic equivalency of trees and landscaping is not easy and it is not dependent on simple arithmetic calculations. Professional plant appraisal is a serious undertaking that requires both a depth of knowledge and expert judgments. This is especially important when that question or problem pertains to the amenity or **aesthetic** qualities that a tree or landscape element provides to its owner. While this is not an easy question to answer, it is a question for which PAs are supremely qualified and equipped to provide an unambiguous answer.

A 2015 Harris survey conducted for the National Association of Landscape Professionals indicated that 75% of Americans felt that having a home with a yard was important and that for 90% of those who have a yard, it is important to keep that yard well maintained. Beyond this encouraging number, fully 91% of Americans felt it was important that their home be near trees, grass or nice landscapes. The same survey says that 84% of home buyer decisions would be affected by the quality of the landscaping of a home. In my own experience, trees can often be the single most important element in the decision to buy a home. I cannot count all the times a client has told me "we bought this house because of that tree" or "my wife loved this tree, so we decided on this house" or "I had a tree like that in my yard growing up, so I bought this property."

According to the USDA Agriculture Statistics Board's September 2007 report, Americans spent nearly $4.65 billion on nursery plants alone in 2006. Of course, this only includes the plants themselves and does not include the labor, other materials, equipment, transportation costs and profits involved in putting those plants into the landscape. These costs and profit would add another two to seven times the plant costs, bringing the total to somewhere between ~$9 and $23.5 billion spent annually on installing plants alone. While Americans spent around $40 billion on turf maintenance and care, the total American landscaping bill came in around $60 billion — and that was over ten years ago. That figure will likely eclipse $100 billion today. At the time of this writing in 2017, there were 321.4 million people living in 117 million households in the United States. Eighty percent of these households had landscaping and they spend about $1,028.00 per household on it. And they do it every year. Americans invest about 2% of their annual income into their landscaping (it's actually about 4% if you own the land) and their trees represent a large portion of that expenditure. The numbers are far greater than most people think — I know because I've asked them. People are constantly surprised by how much time and money they spend on something they care about, but they are not necessarily conscious of the costs. I think that is why people are sometimes surprised at how much they regard trees when they are gone and they are even more surprised at the actual costs to replace them when they are lost.

Americans spend more money on turfgrasses maintenance than all other landscape elements combined.

As a real estate investment, professional landscaping consistently ranks among the top five on returns for your money. *USA Today*, *Forbes* and *Money* magazine have all published articles that speak to this. Professionally designed and executed landscaping is one of the best investments you can make in your home and a variety of research studies have consistently shown that it can produce up to 20% greater equity in a home property value on the open market. I have personally experienced this in my own home, where I spent about $5,000 on the planning and execution and then received another $15,000 in equity — albeit I did much of the work myself. There is significant value in trees and that value can be quantified, calculated and priced appropriately. In summary, there is a large pool of buyers and sellers in the real estate markets who place a high value on properties that contain trees and landscaping as elements of value, where trees and landscaping are considered improved elements to the land. There is also plenty of evidence to suggest that homes with large mature trees and landscaping bring far greater value to a property than homes with new landscaping and smaller, younger trees.

So, real estate appraisers, (**REA**s) real estate brokers and the real estate market participants all agree. Trees and landscaping improve property value. Ask the question simply and you will get a simple "Yes, trees and landscaping make a positive difference." But ask the same question a little differently and you will get another answer altogether. Ask how much the trees and landscaping are worth in terms of monetary value and you will get a look of bewilderment. REAs often get uncomfortable with a question like that. You can see their eyes gloss over, their hands begin to twitch and they begin to sidestep the question in various ways. The reason is simple: Most residential real estate appraisal problems (those appraisals that are performed for a government backed mortgage) do not require a thorough evaluation and analysis of the landscaping. There is simply no repository of ready and reliable comparative sales data points on trees and landscaping. That information simply does not exist. Some claim that you can do some very sophisticated regression analysis from some far away data sets of disparate properties to inform value, but that is not real estate appraisal. That is hocus pocus, abracadabra and poof — out from the wizard's curtain comes a number that sounds good. Real estate appraisal requires reliable, relevant (local) and substantive comparative sales data points in order to solve comparative sales (market) problems. When no market data is available, cost is a suitable substitute for developing an opinion value; cost is good when market value cannot be performed credibly.

Cost is reliable and credible because cost data about the relevant characteristics of the property is plentiful, local and true. Since all of the real estate rulebooks say that when you don't have adequate sales comparison data points (like size, species, placement and condition of trees), the appraiser may use income approach or cost approach. In most PAL assignments, cost will be used. When it comes to most amenity trees, the only reliable and credible alternative approach to comparative sales is cost and cost data is plentiful. REAs typically lack the necessary skills and knowledge that are needed to develop costs for amenity trees and landscaping. They simply do not have the knowledge and experience to evaluate and analyze the size, species, location and condition of trees and other plants. REAs typically cannot give a coherent answer to the question of how much are the trees worth. Occasionally, a REA will come back with timber value or will quote some obscure, poorly conceived, flimsy or contrived research paper that has been conducted in a far-off land, but these answers are usually meaningless in relevance to answering the question of tree and landscape worth in locally supported context, using current sales data in a reliable and credible way. Fortunately for the real estate appraisal community, there is another community of PAs who are supremely qualified to take on the question and who are available as subject matter experts and consultants.

When appraising real estate in the comparative sales approach, REAs collect, analyze, evaluate and disseminate many points of data from various sources that (when applied over limited geographic area, using a large number of transactions, over a sustained period of time) will, theoretically, guide REAs in development of very reliable value opinions. Many of the opinions about improvements that REAs must form are developed using data from either the construction business or from actual real estate market sales transactions, depending on the relevance of the data to the appraisal problem. This data is available via real estate data service bureaus that compile the comparative sales data and sell the data back to the real estate appraisal community. Some points of real estate data are not readily available through a service bureau. Such instances require the specialized knowledge, training and experience of appraisal specialists. Amenity trees and landscaping are one such land improvement in which the service bureau data is quite limited and REAs are often at an extreme disadvantage (unqualified) to form a reliable opinion of value. In most cases where an authoritative opinion about amenity trees is required, the REA will seek out the services of a PA consultant in the execution of a complex real estate appraisal. Likewise, when the problem to be solved is a real estate market problem, PAs will often seek out the services of a REA in the opposite circumstance. In such a situation, neither the REA nor the PA is an entity unto themselves. They are simply working on individual appraisal components to form a reconciled whole. Value is an opinion of worth and it always depends on a variety of elements that are identified by who, what, why, how and when the opinion is valid — we will look at all these elements in depth.

Four Forces That Affect Value

The basic forces that affect the value of any property are categorized broadly in four areas: physical, economic, governmental and social. These forces may have greater influence roles, depending on the type and definition of value that is sought.

Physical Force

Physical forces that influence plant value include both the physical condition of the subject plant parts being appraised and the physical characteristics of the site that envelops the subject(s). The relevant subject condition issues that arise from the the environment in which the subject of the appraisal is growing is a critical physical attribute that requires a competent understanding. The subject's ability to adapt to the site conditions and the ability of the subject's placement to efficiently deliver on the intended or perceived benefits is critical to plant value. Site history, adaptability of plant species, deficiencies of site character (the presence of toxins, pollution, **exotic plants** or **pests)** are examples of the physical forces that can negatively influence a plant's perceived value. A few external forces that can affect plant perceptions of value include environmental concerns, extremely **hazardous conditions**, **linkages**, **nuisance** issues, stigmatized property and wetlands. Topography, utility **easement** proximity, **soil** conditions, water availability, climate and natural features and barriers can also physically influence plant value.

Economic Force

The economic forces that influence the value of trees are quite dissimilar to those of real estate. With trees, the main economic forces involve the price fluctuations associated with the wholesale supply, distribution, construction costs and demand for trees. As with any production cycle, the production of trees involves a range of inputs and garners pricing at the wholesale and retail distribution levels. These cost inputs, as well as external influences in design and maintenance costs, taxation, inflation, interest rates, labor and transportation all play a role in the cost to plant trees as landscaping.

Governmental Force

There may be a myriad of design and other regulatory limitations that are imposed by the government to control the extent, species selections and placement of plants in a site. Planting requirements may also be precluded for a site's development or general land redevelopment. These restrictions may influence the ability of plants to deliver on their perceived or intended benefits. Utility easements are a common occurrence in areas where amenity trees exist and they can have a dramatic influence on perceived plant values. Zoning regulations can also influence people's perception of value on plants. It is important to know that the **standard of care** and maintenance of trees is higher in real estate zones where dense population results in higher occupancy traffic, and this gives rise to greater concerns of safety and maintenance costs, which can also influence people's perceptions of value.

Social Force

As time passes, people's cultural preferences for land use, landscape design (including style and theme preference) and their demand for certain functional and aesthetic amenity benefits that are produced by trees and plants may change. As these trends follow along with changes in growth, stability, **decline** and revitalization demographics, they can have profound influence on the perceived value of plants and trees as defined in the appraisal problem.

What is Appraisal?

According to the Appraisal Institute, appraisal is the act or systematic process of developing an opinion of value. An appraisal is an opinion of value of or an opinion pertaining to **appraised value** and its related functions, such as appraisal practice or appraisal services. Appraisal requires knowledge, judgment and the ability to systematically apply specific processes and procedures to answer a specific question of worth or a specified range of appraisal problems. An appraisal is the expert estimation of value for some type of property in terms of money. Value is always an opinion and an appraisal is an opinion of value. We must never confuse opinion with fact since facts can be verified and can never change based on judgment. Now, appraisal opinions must rely on facts and those facts are critically important when developing certain opinions about the appraisal problem and in deciding what approaches and procedures should be employed to solve that problem. Suffice it to say, facts are still facts and opinions are not facts — they are opinions. An appraisal is always an opinion based on the relevant facts, and the correct processing of those facts, within the applicable procedures.

What is a Professional Amenity Plant Appraiser?

A professional plant appraiser (PA) is an individual who, through adequate education, training, knowledge and experience, has the necessary skills to competently, independently, impartially and objectively perform PALs in the various circumstances in which amenity plants need to be appraised. The need for plant appraisal is wide and varied, as we saw earlier. This includes residential trees and landscapes, commercial landscapes, public spaces and other amenity plant settings, excluding timber. The PA has depth of knowledge and experience with the species of plants they appraise, plant growth **habit**s and other plant attributes. Plant appraisers are familiar with the appropriate plant placements, uses in the landscape and the various health and structural conditions in which they exist. The PA is able to identify the anticipated benefits that trees produce and is skilled in identifying how those benefits are perceived/received by people. In short, plant appraisers know what makes amenity trees and plants desirable.

One of the principles of professional plant appraisal is competence. Only through the time and experience of observing tree defects/maladies and their impacts under a wide range of circumstances can the PA adequately develop the skills needed to objectively judge tree conditions. This critical judgment requires that the PA know the anatomy of trees intimately, know the difference between normal and symptomatic conditions and know how defects or maladies will affect the useful life of the plant in the delivery of aesthetic and functional benefits to its owner. The PA must also anticipate the short and long-term effects of maladies, defects, or deficiencies and the extent to which they may be cured. Critical to appraising the value of plants, it is important for the PA to be familiar with the cost of any curative task so that it can be estimated credibly and reliably.

What is Property?

There are basically three types of property: **real property** (land and all that is permanently attached to it), personal property (things that are not attached to land) and intellectual property (things that are copyrighted, trademarked or patented). Real property can also be categorized into two distinct types: 1)the "dirt", or land, and 2) the improvements to the land. The improvements may be thought of as any elements of value that are not dirt. Even the dirt may have special value if the dirt has special characteristics that may be mined and taken for other uses, such as coal, quarry materials, **mineral** deposits, etc. Normally, though, dirt is dirt and is neither taken away nor added to create new land. Improvements, however, can be made to the land. Most improvements to the land make the land more valuable under various circumstances. Home builders, for example, often speculate that they can build a residential home on a piece of land for less money (at cost) than a home will command on the open market, thus making the real property more valuable and (hopefully) profitable. In fact, one of the measurements of the market value for land improvements is the cost to build the improvement. Of course, some improvements may be of such unique character and of such small demand that no buyer could ever be found. While most homes that are built are sold within a **reasonable** time frame, this is not always the case. Sometimes speculation houses are built (for various reasons) at greater costs than they can command in the market, resulting in a speculation loss.

Speculation homes are built because homebuilders are speculating that they will be able to build homes for less cost than they can command at market pricing. This is not always the case as costs sometimes (for various reasons) overrun the market prices.

Since trees and landscaping are usually well attached to the land and since trees/landscaping can be quite difficult to detach from the land, they are usually considered real property in real estate transactions. There are also many situations in which trees are evaluated as being apart from the land or as improvements to the land. This is certainly true in the landscape contracting business in which trees are bought and sold in the marketplace and contracts are executed for transporting trees from a nursery, **transplanting** into someone's landscape and optionally guaranteed for a period. In this type of transaction, the **establish**ed tree that has been purposefully planted is considered an improved element of the land. A tree improvement may be valued in context with the remainder of a real property (the land and all the improvements) or the costs of transporting and transplanting the personal property tree may be applicable to the appraisal problem. As a separate land element, costs are added to the remainder of the real property as a separate opinion of value when used to inform an opinion for the entire real property.

Since real property appraisal in the United States is often used in government-backed financial instruments, such as Fannie Mae, Freddy Mac, FHA and VA loans, federal and state licensure of real estate appraisal is a carefully governed institution and may involve statutory regulations over many aspects of this market type and definition of real estate appraisal. Strict adherences to the Uniform Standards of Professional Appraisal Practice (USPAP, which is written and authored by the authority of the U.S. Congress) is required for any U.S. government-backed real estate loans. This does not apply to appraisals that are not affiliated with government loans and that fall under other institutional relationships and instruments. For most purposes, professional plant appraisal will not involve government backing and professional plant appraisals do not fall under the same real estate licensure limits and regulations as government-backed mortgage appraisals.

Geographic Jurisdictional Authority

While the United States does not have federal statutory regulations regarding the practice of PAL, some state and local authorities have developed ordinances and laws that dictate the value of plants and trees under a variety of circumstances. The PA should be aware of and understand these laws and how to apply them since these laws will take precedence over any other appraisal data or collective methods, practices and procedures when state or local statutes are applicable. Attorneys are a great resource for understanding and interpretation of the law.

The professional amenity plant appraisal consists of a series of procedures that begin with the identification of the appraisal problem and end with the transmission of the opinion of value to the client. Within this process, there is the scope of work or work plan that is needed to limit data collection activities and analysis activities that support the appraiser's opinion of value. Finally, the appraiser reports their opinion in one of several formats. The flow chart in Chapter Two outlines the appraisal process.

CHAPTER TWO

Appraisal Problem Identification

To form an objective and independent opinion of value in an appraisal problem, we must first clearly define the type and definition of the value about which we will form an opinion. The type and definition of value serves as the purpose of the appraisal opinion. The type of value sought in the work of the appraisal (which is also the purpose of the appraisal) will be derived by anticipating the needs of the people who will use the appraisal. That means the data that is mined to support your opinion of value must be appropriate to the type value you are seeking. When executed, the type of value sought and the data that is analyzed are directly accountable for the reliability/credibility of the value opinion. If a cost type value is sought, then cost data must be used. If market value is sought, market data must be used and so on. The people identified in the appraisal problem consist of the owner of the property, the client (who may or may not be the owner), the users of the appraisal and the jurisdictional authority. The type and definition of value that is permitted in any appraisal assignment is determined by the type and definition of value that the jurisdictional authority will allow.

Since there are a myriad of possible practices and procedures involved in the development of an opinion for any type and definition of value, the type and definition of value sought must be specific to an appraisal's use in practice. Defining value depends on an understanding of what the relevant facts are and how the relevant facts (characteristics data) may be analyzed to obtain a reliable conclusion of value. The type and definition of value sought, the use of the appraisal and the scope of work involved serve to steer the investigation into the discovery of relevant facts and data. The facts that are researched and discovered within the scope of work support and guide the appraiser to judge their relevance in the specific type(s) and definition(s) of value that is/are sought, in a demonstrably reputable, credible and reliable way. The facts and data that are obtained and analyzed should be the facts that best represent/support the economic model(s) that most credibly and reliably fulfill the need for the appraisal. It is up to the appraiser to be independent and impartial when investigating, analyzing and judging the relevant facts.

The users of the appraisal are generally faced with making some sort of decision and that decision will be informed by the appraiser's opinion. That opinion must be informed by the data and fact patterns that are uncovered within the assignment scope of work. The fact patterns must, by necessity, support the defined type and definition of value that is sought in appraisal assignment. Sometimes this creates a conflict between what is needed to complete the assignment and what the relevant facts will permit. In a situation where there is a conflict between the scope of work that is needed to solve the appraisal problem and what the client will allow, the appraiser must be permitted to use the appropriate scope of work that the fact patterns require or withdraw from the appraisal assignment. When called upon to do so, the appraiser must be prepared to defend his or her value opinions and the work that went into forming that opinion must be defensible. When withdrawing from an assignment, the appraiser may be called upon to defend the reasons why.

The Professional Amenity Plant Appraisal Process

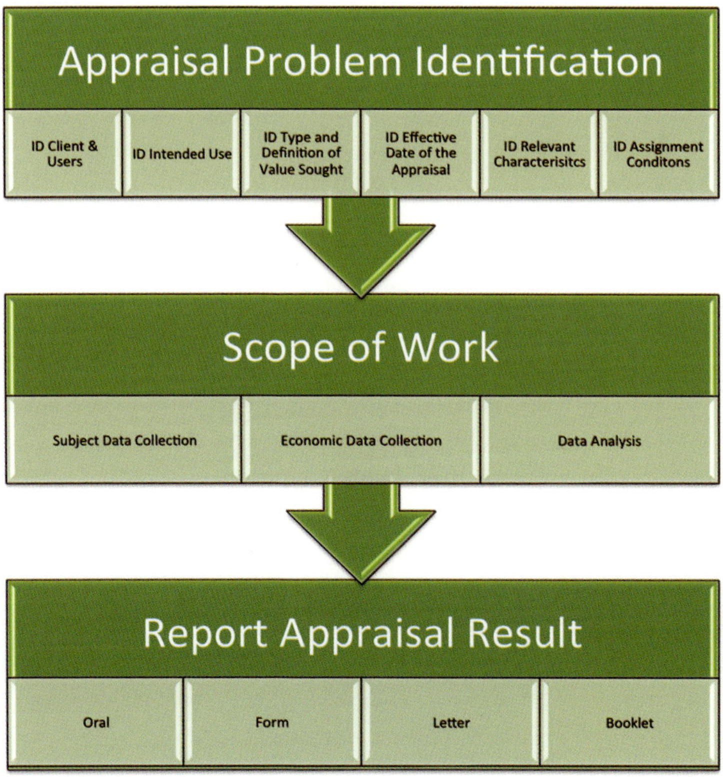

Elements of the Appraisal Problem

The appraisal problem consists of several elements, each of which provides framework or scaffolding to the appraisal problem. These elements are the people involved, the use for which the type and definition of value is needed, the effective date of the appraisal, the relevant characteristics (facts and data) of the subject property that are needed to solve the appraisal problem, any permissible conditions that are placed on the assignment and any extraordinary assumption or hypothetical constructs that are necessarily employed to complete the assignment.

Identify the Client and Intended Users

The client is the person or entity that engages you to perform the appraisal. The client is always, by necessity, a user of the appraisal. The client engages the appraiser, but the client need not necessarily be the person or entity who pays for the appraisal. In the same vain, the type of user and/or the users of the appraisal need to be clearly identified for the appraisal problem ID to be complete. In a **forensic** assignment, for example, one of the uses is always legal proceedings and one of the users, aside from the client, is the court. In any assignment, it is helpful for the appraiser to assume the independent disposition of working for all the users of the appraisal and not just the client only.

Identify the Intended Use

Professional plant appraisal is often the basis of economic decisions regarding plants. What those decisions will be are at the heart of how the appraisal will be used. The key identifier of how an appraisal will be used is portrayed in the type of data that is appropriate to the defined type and definition of value sought. The data mined in the scope of work is outlined as the appraisal work progresses. The depth and scope of research that are permitted are agreed upon by both the client and the appraiser. That data is then garnered by the appraiser and the type and depth of analysis is necessarily incorporated into the defined appraisal results. Since the intended use (and the type and definition of value) determines the type and extent of data and facts that must be obtained within the appraiser's scope of work, the intended use requires a minimal level of work to be credible. This minimum level of work is conveyed to the client by the appraiser and is determined by the appraiser's assessment of what is needed to credibly solve the type and definition of value that is sought. The appraiser determines the minimum scope of work that is needed to credibly solve the problem for the intended use. The appraiser works with the client to determine the maximum scope of work and communicates the pros and cons of each level of limitation.

Some uses of amenity plant appraisal:

- Litigation
- Insurance binders
- Asset portfolio management
- Property loss tax deductions
- Property donation tax deduction
- Highest and best use for real estate appraisal
- CREMV in condemnation of land
- Before and after casualty loss assessments
- Other needs

Purpose of Assignment (Type of Value)

The purpose of the appraisal is defined by the type and definition of value that is sought. While it may be easy to confuse the intended use with the purpose of the appraisal they are necessarily distinct. The purpose of an appraisal is to form an opinion of value for a defined type of value, which represents an economic aspect or model of the subject being appraised. Regardless of the value type requested, the type and definition of value employed by the PA must always be appropriate and reliable for the intended use for all the users and must not simply be advantageous to the client only.

The type and definition of value sought will also be important in the work of the PA in that it guides the type and extent of data that is garnered and the types and extent of analysis that will take place in the appraisal process. This may affect the scope of work that the appraisal will encompass. It is important to note that real estate market problems differ considerably from certain land improvement problems like trees and landscaping because the available real estate service bureau data for trees (apart from other land elements of value) is quite scarce and notoriously unreliable. While it may theoretically be possible to glean CREMV from some market transactions by using hypothetical conditions, (they would have to be wildly speculative) and the mathematics and research to do so in practice is prohibitively expensive. Using such an approach would also result in an unreliable and very speculative plant appraisal opinion. Cost data from the landscape construction markets are readily available to PAs and are very reliable. In nearly all cases, an REA performing CREMV of trees will need to employ a PA with the necessary training, skills and experience to develop a cost approach type of value for the tree and landscape improvements. Using the complex approach (by employing Market Approach for most of the real estate elements, *and* using Cost Approach for landscaping improvements) informs the appraisal user of the REA's opinion and of the PA's opinion of value as a reconciled whole.

Identify the Effective Date

There are many dates associated with an appraisal that will be important for record-keeping purposes, but the most important date is the effective date of the appraisal. The effective date is required to establish the time context of the opinion of value. This is the date on which the value is good; for example, in a tort damages case, two effective dates will be important: the date just prior to the damage and the last date on which the actual damage occurred as a basis for establishing a before and after loss estimate. In some cases, like chemical trespass damages, several appraisals may be performed over time to determine a trend of what may be expected in the future. These are just a couple of examples that show how the effective date may provide context to the value opinion. In addition to the effective date, there is also the date of assignment, the date of site inspection, and the date of the report, which are essential recordkeeping elements of an appraisal. It may also be important to record the date that the appraisal is transmitted to the client.

Amenity plant appraisal assignments may be retrospective value (in the past, based on past conditions), current value (based on current conditions), or they may be prospective value at some point in the future. Prospective values are questionable since there are many factors that can affect the value of trees and no one can predict exactly what will happen to a tree or what the conditions will be in the future.

Identify the Relevant Characteristics

The relevant characteristics of a tree, site or the landscape have direct bearing on their value. These characteristics can be broadly categorized into four distinct areas: size, species, condition and location. Each of these areas requires specialized knowledge, skill and training to credibly identify, qualify, quantify and judge in an independent and objective manner. While real estate appraisal includes judgments about the physical characteristics and the legal status of a property, oftentimes the legal status of amenity tree improvements goes unexamined by PAs. Plant appraisers (PAs) are primarily concerned with the physical, economic and governmental forces that influence the opinion of value and any obsolescence contained in those forces. While PAs may form opinions and give testimony about relevant legal matters (particularly those opinions and conclusions related to governmental forces influencing plant value), most matters of a legal nature are best left to legal experts and for others to judge. Unless qualified to do so, professional plant appraisers must never offer legal counsel or legal advice to clients.

Assignment Conditions

Sometimes there are important conditions of an assignment that must be conveyed to the users to protect the appraiser from errors or omissions in their work product and they serve to inform the client of constraints to which a value opinion is limited. For example, if a tree is placed in a location that prevents a portion from being examined during a site visit, it is important to explain what could not be seen during the examination since what could not be seen may contain elements that would otherwise affect an opinion of value. This would be a limiting condition of the assignment. If you see an overhead wire and you think that there may have been a **pruning** event in the past that is obscured by vegetation, that would be another condition that would need to be explained within the appraisal problems identification. There are also other considerations. For example, if the report is for litigation purposes, a condition of the assignment may be that there will be no testimony unless the client agrees to pay for the time in court. Another example is in the collection of nursery sales data. If the data was not verified through actual sales transaction receipts, the appraiser may wish to issue a disclaimer stating that nursery catalogue pricing was used to determine nursery product sales prices. It is also a good idea to copyright any intellectual work that is yours alone to prevent unauthorized persons from recording and using your work without permission.

Extraordinary Assumptions

An extraordinary assumption is any assumption, if found to be false, that might alter the appraiser's opinion. Assumptions may be used as a tool to aid the PA in the development of credible results in many types of assignments, especially where a limited scope of work prohibits the exhaustive testing or verification of facts. In such a case, the appraiser must clearly state the extraordinary assumption that, if it is found to be false, the opinion of value may need to be reformed in some way. This is often the case when the property in question is assumed to be owned **fee**

simple and without encumbrances of any kind. If found to be false, this factor may alter the appraiser's opinion. Similarly, not all tree **defects** can be detected with visual observation or **sounding**. In this limited capacity, an appraiser may assume that there are no major internal defects and may appraise the value of a tree with a limited understanding, so long as that limited understanding is clearly stated in the opinion.

Hypothetical Conditions

Occasionally, a professional plant appraisal assignment requires the consideration of a "what if" scenario when the opinion of value is subject to specific speculation measures or arrangements. Hypothetical conditions are a specific assignment element that is related to a condition that is contrary to what is known to exist by the appraiser at the effective date of the appraisal. This is sometimes a necessary tool that is used to fulfill specific speculative assignment criteria. For example, nursery business trend models are sometimes employed to develop and project future sales for a variety of species as the maturity windows of a crop begin to close, necessitating a culling decision at some point in the future. In doing so, the client needs to anticipate future demand and returns of an investment in the nursery crop space and needs to know when the time will be right to cull the over-mature crop and replant with a new crop. In this situation, a hypothetical scenario of future plant sales is projected within the appraisal result.

Scope of Work

Once the appraisal problem has been identified, the next step in the appraisal process is to plan out the scope of the work involved in solving the problem. The scope of work (SOW) determines to what extent the appraiser will go to develop a credible and reliable opinion of value. Think of the SOW as a planned outline of the work that will be performed during an appraisal assignment. This plan is used for all work involved in producing the appraisal and is the basis for communicating with the client to determine the budget needed to fulfill the assignment. The SOW is useful in determining how much time or what fees will be necessary to produce the final work product. Each appraisal assignment is unique and will include all the essential information that pertains to the appraisal problem. The SOW in professional plant appraisal includes things like the level of detail to which the subject will be examined and studied; the type and amount of data that will be mined, researched or acquired; and the extent of testing and analysis that will be applied to solve the type and definition of value that is sought.

The SOW is calculated by taking all the information that informs the appraisal problem and deciding what it will take to solve that problem. This is by no means at the sole discretion of the PA. The scope of work upper limit is a fully collaborative effort between the needs of the client (including any use or budget constraints), the requirements of the problem and the judgments of the PA. The SOW must also be flexible throughout the appraisal process since the process often uncovers new information that may necessarily change the type and amount of work that will be needed to solve the problem. The scope of work is communicated between the client and the appraiser and is mutually agreed upon. There are limitations, however, that are important for the PA to consider. The PA must not allow the client to so limit the scope of work that it prevents the appraiser from producing a credible and reliable assignment result. Similarly, the appraiser must be flexible enough to meet the client's budgetary constraints, but the appraiser must not take on an assignment that has a predetermined result or outcome. The PA's results must always be independent and free from the client's bias or wants. From time to time, the wants of the client may not be reconciled to the minimum needs of the assignment scope of work. In such situations, the PA must withdraw.

As the appraisal process progresses, the information uncovered may warrant a change in the type and/or amount of data to be collected, or there may be changes in the way the data is analyzed, tested, researched or reported. When increased work changes are necessary, they are communicated to the client and the client and appraiser collaboratively determine the new SOW boundaries. In the case of landscaping, there are often encumbrances that infringe on a property owner's right (to the greatest extent possible) to use the vegetation growing on land. Things, such as public **utility** lines, are often in conflict with growing trees. Since a utility owner usually has a mandated **right-of-way vegetation management easement** contract to trim trees and prevent them from interfering with the facility, knowing that fact will limit the tree in certain ways and those limits will influence the perception of tree value. The initial SOW may not specify that the easement contract language be researched and evaluated, but as the appraisal process progresses, that specific language may become important as more relevant facts are uncovered. Another example would be when the SOW for an appraisal is determined prior to the site examination and, during the site examination, a previously unknown and large defect is observed that could potentially cause the tree to be hazardous, but to determine the tree's hazard status, the tree needs to be carefully tested for the extent of decay. In this case, the appraiser communicates with the client and discusses the defect and its potential implications for the appraisal. The appraiser and client mutually decide on the best course forward.

Scope of Work and Intended User

PAs are hired by clients who intend to use their appraisal for a specific purpose. While a client is always a user, there may be other users, like the courts or another interested party of a transaction. The intended user(s) may be identified as individuals, entities or another type of user. The scope of work in PAL must be sufficient to form a reliable and credible opinion of value for the intended user or type of user.

Scope of Work, Type and Definition of Value

In PAL, it is the type of anticipated amenity benefits contained in the right of ownership of plants that chiefly drives the consideration of the type and definition of value sought. In all cases, the value sought must be a defined type of value. The defined type of value must also be credible in terms of the data used and the appraisal must be performed ethically. Depending on the specific assignment scope of work, each of the relevant characteristics is analyzed in detail (according to how value is defined) and judged as to relevance in the appraisal process. Each relevant characteristic is also judged regarding its status in terms of obsolescence of benefit delivery. The scope of work must be extensive enough to allow the appraiser to obtain sufficient amounts of data about the relevant characteristics of the subject to support a credible opinion of value. In comparative sales approach to amenity plant value, it means obtaining enough local sales data points about the size, species, condition and placement of plant contributions to the real estate sale transactions. In income approach, it is obtaining enough actual sales data points for the sales of trees or increased rents and generated income that has resulted from the amenity trees. In cost approach, it is obtaining enough relevant cost data inputs and calculating all plant benefit depreciations to those costs.

Scope of Work Relevant Characteristics

The relevant characteristics of plants are vast and involve both internal characteristics (such as the condition of each plant part and the species of the plant) and external characteristics such as the landscape placement, site conditions, climate and soil where the subject plant(s) grow(s). Ultimately, the plant appraiser must be able to credibly judge how well the relevant characteristics of the plant provide the relevant benefits that are sought, enjoyed or anticipated by the landscape user, that is the owner, a prospective seller, or a prospective buyer. The appraiser judges how well users can anticipate the benefits from the relevant plant characteristics. The relevant characteristics of plant appraisals are those characteristics that are the source or limitations of the anticipated benefits, the benefits themselves and any deficiencies in the ability of the physical plant parts to deliver. The data about those benefits and characteristics is directly related to the cost to produce or replace them. The scope of work in examining the relevant characteristics should be comprehensive enough to meet the user's needs.

Scope of Work and Data Collection

The type and amount of data that a PA may obtain and analyze in the professional plant appraisal process can be extensive and the cost of exhaustive data capture and analysis can be very expensive. The appraiser must decide upon the minimum relevant data points that must be collected, analyzed and calculated to produce a credible appraisal result. The appraiser and the client communicate and decide on the amount and extent of work that the appraiser will go through in obtaining credible data and, together, they decide the upper scope of work limits that will be performed to produce a credible result. Ethically, an appraiser must not allow a client to so limit the scope of work as to prevent the appraiser from producing a credible, reliable and impartial appraisal result.

The plant appraiser may consult a variety of sources of information on a regular basis. Public domain, data from personal files, appraisal software, bibliographical references and information databases may all provide relevant facts and data points from which PAs may draw support for their opinions of value. Some facts are more relevant and reliable than others and the PA must be able to use sound judgment and defensible reasoning when weighing, calculating and processing their opinions of value. While other tools may be very helpful in forming an opinion of value, the appraiser's own investigation, examination and site observations of the subject's relevant internal and external characteristics are of chief importance.

The type and extent of data collection is a critical component of the SOW. The size, location, species and condition of a tree are critical to the benefits that a tree produces to users/owners, regardless of type and definition of value sought. These elements need to be known and understood by the PA in detail before they are analyzed for value. The level of detail contained in the obtained data pool may vary somewhat from assignment to assignment, but the level of detail must be great enough to permit a credible appraisal result.

In tort damage claims of civil wrong, the PA must ascertain the conditions of the plant being appraised before the act of damage occurred and the conditions of the plant after an act of wrong. The resulting difference in extracting the pre-damaged condition to the post-damaged condition determines the amount of appraised value loss. There are many factors to consider and great care must be taken to investigate any claim of loss. Some types of evidence, such as photographs taken prior to the damage, historical aerial imagery, maintenance records and other preexisting documentation about a subject plant offers reliable proof of preexisting conditions, while statements of the owner, testimonial of a neighbor, or commentary by previous owners may be less reliable as proof.

Likewise, it is critically important that the PA obtain facts and data that are independent of potential conflicts of interest and that they are gathered in an unbiased manner. The most reliable way to obtain objective and independent observations is to examine the plants, take measurements and take photographs yourself, independently. When this is not possible, the appraiser may bring another qualified, independent and objective professional in to make observations, take photos, take measurements and examine the subject plants. Likewise, the gathering of support data, such as estimates and book pricing, should be done independently and objectively, using appropriate sources.

Depending on the SOW involved in the appraisal, additional testing and analysis may be warranted to more precisely determine conditions and the extent of damage and to evaluate any safety risk concerns and/or to evaluate tree health and structure. Drilling resistance technology, **tomography**, radar technology, remote sensing equipment, normalized difference vegetation indexing (**NDVI**), chlorophyll florescence and other measures have all been used effectively to analyze the structural elements and health of live trees. Since tort damage cases often end up in court, the PA must be at least familiar with these important assessment tools and be able to properly discuss their relevance and reliability limits for use in a legal setting. If the appraiser needs the results but does not possess the requisite training or skills to use such technology credibly or reliably, the appraiser has three choices: 1) hire it done by a qualified individual, 2) acquire the necessary training and skills, or 3) decline the assignment.

An increment bore may be used to take core samples of wood tissue. This core sample was taken to analyze the growth rate and age of a very large and very old burr oak tree.

Sampling and laboratory analysis may also be included in the SOW to perform **dendrochronological** analysis, insect identification, disease identification and soil analysis. The plant appraiser must know the proper sampling techniques and protocols for obtaining relevant samples and must be competent to perform the forensic handling of the samples. The appraiser must also be able to interpret the results of any testing or any lab report reliably.

Dr. Julian Dunster's book *Documenting Evidence Practical Guidance for Arborists* provides a wealth of information on the process and pitfalls of collecting and storing evidential data for all types of assignments, including those for use in the PAL process. (Dunster, 2014)

Identifying Relevant Plant Characteristics

In the professional amenity plant appraisal process, the relevant characteristics are identified and the data from these characteristics are gathered within the scope of work of the assignment. The relevant characteristics and data facts are gathered and recorded in sufficient quantity to enable the appraiser to solve the appraisal problem and form an opinion that is credible and reliable. This is much easier said than done in execution. Part of what makes plant appraisal challenging is deciding which characteristics are relevant and which are not. The amenity plant appraisal characteristics listed in this book are commonly used but all characteristics are not relevant for every appraisal assignment. Only a fraction of those characteristics identified in this book will be applicable to any particular appraisal problem. Of the vast array of characteristics I have compiled here, the PA will have to pick and choose which ones are appropriate for a given assignment scope and which are not.

This resource offers descriptions and details about many characteristics that may be used as an aid to identify the anticipated benefits that plants produce, and it offers a wide array of characteristics that may affect how well a plant is able to deliver on those anticipated benefits. Think of the identification chapters as though you are at the buffet line of a cafeteria and you need to fill a plate for someone who is sitting with you. As a plant appraiser your client has a need and the user of your appraisal has a need. They both need you to solve the appraisal problem in a credible and reliable way. In any given appraisal assignment, you will have to decide which characteristics are relevant and what data you will need acquire and analyze to solve the problem. You may only need to use a half-dozen characteristics for a rudimentary assignment or you may need to identify and evaluate dozens of characteristics to fulfill the assignment. The idea here is to provide a smorgasbord of characteristics for you to pick and choose to solve the type and definition of value you identify in the appraisal problem. Take what you need and leave what you don't out of your investigation. In time, you will likely take on an expanded and varied breadth of assignments that allow you to explore an ever-widening range of relevant plant characteristics and benefits.

Site suitability pertains to the uninhibited ability of a plant to perform its useful aesthetics and functions and be able to deliver its benefits to the intended landscape user/owner. There are many site characteristics that may be examined to determine how suitably a site enables a subject plant species to fully deliver the benefits it can produce. Oftentimes, however the delivery of the benefits to the user/owner is diminished by one or more of the site characteristics that are external to the subject. The PA distinguishes the relevant site characteristics and the relevant benefits delivered and judges any limitations of benefit delivery toward the intended landscape design purposes.

Purpose and Use of Trees

Landscape trees and plants have two basic types of uses. There are functional uses (which are easily measured) and there are aesthetic uses that are designed to evoke a feeling of some kind. Both kinds of uses are important in professional amenity plant appraisal.

In a PAL, amenity trees and plants are considered an element of improvement to the land on which they grow. This is true regardless if the tree was planted or if it grew naturally. That is because it is in the anticipated benefits and/or liabilities that are produced, perceived or received that give them worth or lack of it. Value may be positive or negative, depending on the presence of any liabilities contained in the amenity. To calculate a credible estimation of value, the PA must consider the purposes and uses for which the amenity tree is perceived to be valuable; that is, the amenity tree benefits that a tree produces is the beginning of the opinion of amenity tree value. Consideration must be given to how well trees provided those amenity benefits to their owner as they are or may be perceived. When damage is involved, plant appraisers must also consider the extent of the damage and how the functional and aesthetic amenity tree benefits were affected. In all cases, the plant appraiser must also collect the appropriate data that informs how the relevant characteristics of trees contribute to plant performance in delivery of the amenity benefits and their effectiveness in contributing to amenity tree's worth.

Exclusive Owner Benefits

An exclusive benefit is any appreciable quality that a thing may produce for its owner that, if not for the fundamental nature of the thing, the appreciable quality would not exist. The owner of the thing is lawfully permitted to anticipate the unencumbered enjoyment of any appreciable qualities by virtue of his/her rights of ownership in the thing. Plants and trees produce a wide range of benefits and they fulfill a broad range of uses in the landscape. The PA should possess a thorough knowledge and understanding of landscape plants and their uses in landscape architectural design. The PA should also know the principles of landscape design and know how both form and function are used to enhance the benefits that a landscape is able to deliver to its rightful owner. It is important for plant appraisers to focus on exclusive benefits since owners may only have exclusive rights to anticipate enjoyment of benefits that they exclusively own.

General Benefits Produced

A general benefit is any appreciable quality of a thing that may produce to the general public, beyond that which is exclusive to the enjoyment by its owner. Trees and plants are physically owned, but some of the benefits they produce cannot be enjoyed exclusively by their owner. For example, plants produce oxygen in the atmosphere, certainly a benefit to all who breathe.

This benefits the owner, but it also benefits others who breathe the oxygen produced by the tree. Another example would be the morning shade that a tree produces, causing a tree owner's house to be cooler in the summer months, reducing the owner's cooling bill. The same tree casting a shadow on the neighbor's house in the afternoon is not an exclusive benefit to the owner. Reducing the neighbors cooling bill and making the neighbor's home more comfortable does not extend a right for a tree owner to charge a fee for the benefits his neighbor receives from the tree. In most situations of general benefits, the neighbor enjoying the benefits of a not-owned tree has no rights to those benefits. Likewise, the owner of the tree has no right to demand from the neighbor a fee for the general benefits supplied. This principle does not diminish in any way the right of a tree owner to fully enjoy all the exclusive benefits that the owner receives from his/her own tree.

Measuring Tree Size

One of the most straightforward characteristics of plants is size. Measuring size characteristics in the early days had been a source of disconti-

When measuring the cut stump of a tree, it is important to note the height at which the stump is measured. The appraiser needs to account for the difference between the diameter at stump height and the diameter at breast height (DBH).

nuity among plant appraisers, but GPAs 8 and 9 brought a great deal of conformity to measuring the size of tree trunks and they do an excellent job of describing the proper standard of measuring tree trunks in appraisal. It is beyond the scope of this text to add any refinements to trunk measurement data beyond those established in GPA9 guidance.

Trunk measurements, however, are only one type of measurement that indicates a size-to-benefit equivalent to nursery stock. Two other means of measuring tree size have gained wider use since the advent of Google Earth, Bing and other public domain sources of historical aerial imagery. These measurement equivalents are drip area (canopy area) and canopy volume. Canopy areas can be ascertained by examining the outline of a canopy and using either a planimeter to calculate area or by using Google Earth Pro Polygon Tools to calculate area. Also, canopy volume may be measured by calculating the various canopy elements of spherical geometry as first described by Joe Samnik (ISA Conference 2017). Likewise, nursery stock canopies can be measured at the nursery.

CHAPTER THREE

Identification of Species/ Site Suitability Characteristics

Species/site suitability data will be used to analyze and assess how well a plant is able to deliver its benefits to users based on the limitations imposed by the site/species selection characteristics of the landscape architectural design. Plants may suffer physical deterioration and poor health performance for a variety of reasons. Many of those reasons can be traced back to the site conditions being deficient to the species of plant that was selected in the landscape architectural design. Sometimes, that deficiency is an unseen soil characteristic that needs to be tested and identified, or sometimes it is something more visible like poor species selection for the geography or climate. While at times it may not always be possible to pinpoint the root cause of physical deterioration due to scope of work limits, they are listed here if your assignment calls for them.

If the appraiser knows that an obsolescence deficiency exists in species/ site suitability (in terms of plant selection in the design), the appraiser may need to analyze how much obsolescence this deficiency causes. When scope of work limits the ability to test some of these site characteristics, they can generally (not specifically) be identified as physical deterioration of the plant since poor site suitability usually results in some sort of physical deterioration and poor site conditions will limit a plant's health and vitality.

Landscape plants are often forced to live in conditions that are not ideal to their species preference. Some plant species, like pear *(Pyrus sp.)* species, are extremely **adaptable** over a broad range of site conditions while others, like *Franklinia*, serviceberry *(Amelanchier sp.)* and Sassafras *(Sassafras albidum)*, can be quite finicky and difficult to transplant. The precise range of conditions in which a plant will grow is highly dependent on species, so much so that it is really a site/species characteristic. The plant appraiser is greatly assisted to be informed on those sites where plants will thrive and be able to deliver their anticipated benefits well and where there are deficiencies in the site characteristics. When evaluating the relevant characteristics of a site to the plant species:

- the plant appraiser identifies the site characteristics to the species in sufficient detail that they may be reasonably perceived in use by the plant to provide benefits to an owner or interested party;
- the plant appraiser identifies any site characteristic deficiencies in that benefit role, evaluates the effectiveness limits imposed on the plant by the site and then assigns that deficiency as either a site obsolescence or as physical obsolescence (deterioration) to the affected plant parts, but not both;
- and the plant appraiser applies any warranted obsolescence as a weighted deduction for the identified benefit deficiency.

Size to Space

Trees and shrubs continue to grow over time, but as they mature, they tend to grow much more slowly than do juvenile plants. Mature-size plant and tree data is available from a variety of sources and is the benchmark for judging the suitability of plant size to the size limitations that a landscape space may impose. Typically, we think of plants as existing in three dimensions, although they are rarely depicted that way in architectural plans. Trees and shrubs are said to be less suitable to a site where the space allotted is less than the plant's potential mature height and spread. This is because there are higher pruning and other maintenance costs associated with the requirement to keep plants confined to a smaller landscape space than they can naturally grow. The PA should be aware of the mature size of a plant or tree species and be able to judge the suitability of mature plants to the size allotted in a landscape design. This means that when greater disparity exists from the mature plant size to the allotted space, the plant is less suitable and less desirable, and the plant suffers obsolescence. This is a judgment-derived design **deficiency** from 0–100%, 0 being impossible to 100 being no limitation.

Soils and Climate

Each species of plant depends on soil resources for uptake of water and **essential nutrients**. Each species of plant has unique ability to adapt to the various climate conditions and soil types that may exist in a site. While a soil's characteristics may be categorized, measured and analyzed in a myriad of ways, PAs are most interested in those characteristics that affect plant health, **vigor** and **vitality**. For the purpose of keeping the extent in this handbook to the most relevant subject matter of plant appraisals, site conditions have been limited to Site Climate, Soil: Texture, pH, Nutritional Content, **Organic** Content, **Bulk Density**, Soil Biology, Pests and Plant Tolerance. These characteristics are not exhaustive and may, when warranted, be expanded to include other characteristics not covered in this book. It is also important to note that when plant conditions do not exhibit indications of a soil/climate problem, it is customary to assume that no soil/climate problem exists. When the conditions of the plant cause the appraiser to suspect that there is a soil problem, an investigation of soils may become necessary, beginning with the most likely suspects first and moving on to the more remote possibilities until the problem is identified.

While it is not necessary to evaluate each characteristic of the soil or climate for every appraisal problem, it is important to be aware of these characteristics and when they are relevant to the appraisal problem. The appraiser should be able to judge their suitability to the subject for obsolescence when a soil problem exists.

Since each species has varying amounts of adaptability to each of these characteristics, it is important for plant appraisers to know the species adaptive limits of each relevant soil and climatic characteristic. The appraiser will judge the suitability of external characteristics to the internal species characteristics of the subject being appraised. Soil characteristics are most reliably identified through laboratory testing and analysis; however, there are published resources and public domain data sets available that can assist the appraiser with useful information when the scope of work limit prohibits laboratory testing and analysis.

Your local county agricultural extension service is a great resource and the USDA has compiled a large repository of detailed soil information. (USDA, 2013) When using public domain data over laboratory testing and analysis, this limitation should be stated in the scope of work. It is also important to note that climate is a permanent site limitation while soil site limitations or a lack of precipitation may be cured with soil treatment or irrigation.

I have listed these soil and climate characteristics in order of the most common and easily discernable disorders (that also happen to be the least expensive to test, easiest to analyze and easiest to identify) to the least commonly used (the most expensive to test and difficult to analyze and identify):

Climatic Conditions

Climate is the single most important external characteristic that limits plant **physiology**. Some plants can grow over a wide range of climate types while most others are only capable of growing in a narrow range of climate types. *Sunset's Garden Climate Zones* offers a detailed map that includes 45 climatic zones across the United States. The climate characteristics that these zones take into account include the length of growing season, average minimum temperatures, high temperatures, humidity, annual precipitation and wind conditions. These zones characterize climate in a holistic way that accounts for regional distributions and populations of native plant species. Landscape plants are also apt to be either poorly or well suited to those climates. For plant appraisers, this reference is the most relevant and reliable means for identifying climates to which a plant species is best suited; however, few other references have adopted it as a de facto standard in favor of the **USDA Hardiness** Zone Map. Also, the number and variety of plants listed in the *Sunset Garden Zone* map is comparatively limited in scope and it does not lend itself to as broad a range of species as the more comprehensive USDA Hardiness data.

To use climate as a means of determining the suitability of a plant to its growing site, plant appraisers should know about the plant species climate preferences and its adaptability to climes outside of its preferences. The farther a plant grows outside its climatic preference and adaptability, the more maintenance and inputs will be required to allow it to conform. If a plant is located far enough away from its adaptability, it will not perform at all. The plant appraiser may be expected to be capable of judging a plant's suitability to a climate and be able to apply appropriately weighted depreciation deductions to value when climate conditions are less than suitable.

Temperature

The USDA has developed cold **hardiness** temperature ranges for the US. Hardiness Zones and may be used (the USDA has an interactive zone map on their website) as an aid to help appraisers understand minimum cold temperature limits of plants. This map is the most commonly used in practice. Most botanical references give a northern and southern range of zones for which a plant will tolerate temperatures throughout the year. This is a useful characteristic that plant appraisers may use as a consideration of depreciation when plants are growing outside of their USDA Zone preference. Some plants are quite adaptable and many **cultivars** of plants are developed and grown to adapt to climate extremes. The plant appraiser should be able to identify when plants are growing outside of their climatic temperature preferences and be able to judge if a disparity exists. When a disparity exists, the plant appraiser may be expected to make weighted value adjustments in obsolescence.

Soil Moisture

Soil moisture is the leading **limiting factor** for tree health and vitality. Soil water carries all plant nutrients that have dissolved and are absorbed by plants for sustenance. Since no nutrients can enter the tree's internal systems without an abundance of nutrient-rich water, all tree systems are limited and regulated by soil moisture. Water and carbon dioxide are the primary building blocks of photosynthate (carbohydrates), without which no life on earth could exist. Carbohydrates (the product of **photosynthesis** that are produced in the green parts of plants) are the primary component of **cellulose**, **hemicellulose** and **lignin** (all of which are combined by the tree to make woody **tissue**s and all other biochemical and biosynthetic components). Cellulose and hemicellulose make up 99% of a tree's structure. The sugars and starches produced in photosynthesis also provide the fuel that all living plant cells need as food. Trees also absorb water in a process known as evapotranspiration, which cools the tree and provides a mechanism for trees to extract the nutrients they need. (Harris R.J., 2004)

The amount of rainfall that a site receives is one site characteristic that an appraiser can look to as an indicator of soil moisture. The soil's texture, organic content, permeability and **infiltration rate** can have profound effects on the amount of water that is available to plants. Also, plant species have preferences as to how much water is available to them and how often they like to have rainfall or irrigation. Too much water can be just as detrimental to plants as not enough and irrigation can create as many problems for plants as it solves. The plant appraiser should be able to determine if the amount of irrigation and precipitation is appropriate to the soil conditions and if both are suitable for the subject species being appraised. If the soil moisture is not suitable, the plant appraiser should be able to weigh the disparity and be able to judge a weighted obsolescence in value when warranted, being careful to observe that adjustments to irrigation systems can always be made, but the amount of predictable precipitation cannot.

Opposite page: Plants that are adapted to drier climates generally cannot survive climes of higher precipitation. Other plants are adapted to wetter conditions and will not survive without regular watering.

Sunlight/Shade

Sunlight is crucial for photosynthesis, but ornamental plants have been cultivated and adapted for uses based on the amount of sunlight that is available in landscapes and gardens. The amount of sunlight or shade that a plant can tolerate is completely dependent on the plant species. Some landscape spaces have an abundance of direct sunlight all day long while others receive little or no direct sunlight at all. Sun exposure is a vitally important consideration in landscape architectural design and it is one of the chief limiting factors for plant growth, health and vitality. Some plants are highly adaptable to varying light conditions while others are more specialized, requiring either sunny or shaded conditions.

Plants selected for sites that have dense tree **canopy** cover are adapted to shade conditions and these conditions will strictly limit the species of plants that can grow and thrive. Oftentimes, when mature trees have grown to great size and proximity, an apex successional **habitat** can form in which the dense canopy shade completely suppresses under-canopy plant development. In such a site, only the most shade tolerant plants will grow, and they will grow very slowly. If the canopy is removed from such a site, it necessarily changes the variety of plant species that will grow. Increasing sunlight in a mature tree stand will cause undergrowth to develop en masse.

Plant appraisers may be expected to determine when light conditions are suitable for plant growth and vitality and when they are not. The plant appraiser should be able to identify deficiencies or surpluses in sunlight and be able to understand how sunlight exposure will adversely affect plant health and **vigor**. When it is appropriate, the PA may be expected to be capable of calculating appropriately-weighted obsolescence depreciation for sunlight in the appraisal process.

Wind Exposure

Wind and other weather-related events can affect plants structurally, most notably trees. Some trees are well adapted to windy conditions while others are capable of withstanding only moderate wind speeds and gusts. While genetics does play a role in certain aspects of tree structures, some species of trees are better able to adapt to varying wind scenarios. Adaptability is a function of genetics, but generally, with wind exposure and time, tree structures will become better suited to the wind environments in which they grow. Some species are more adaptable and suitable for windy situations than are others. Tree appraisers should be able to identify tree species and tree structures and be able to assess the wind and weather conditions to which a subject tree is exposed. Where there is poor structure and/or species vulnerability to wind events and where weather is likely to cause damage to a subject, the PA may need to judge the potential impacts of damage and the likely extent of damage that would result. If needed, the appraiser may deduct for obsolescence when the risk of wind damage to a tree is very high or likely. The deductions should be weighted with the extent of damage that might be expected due to the poor structure or species selection.

Pests

Nearly all plant species suffer pressures from insects and/or disease. While some plants are susceptible to a large number and variety of pests, others suffer very few incidents of pests. Pest susceptibility is controlled by many factors, the most important of which is the plant's genetic ability to withstand insect and disease pest assaults. Also, the physical condition of plants can also play a role in how well it can fight off insect and disease attacks. Sometimes pests attack en masse in a particular region, greatly increasing the number of attacks that a plant experiences. This results in more pest success than would otherwise exist.

If a known species of plant is growing in an area where certain pests will very likely proliferate (necessitating an increase in maintenance to keep the plant healthy or aesthetically appealing), or if the health conditions of the plant are poor (making it likely the plant will fall prey to pest pressure), then the PA should be aware of both the potential and likelihood of visual/health impacts to the tree. When warranted, a weighted external obsolescence deduction for pest(s) should be calculated in the appraisal process.

Soil pH

Soil **pH** is characteristic that measures how **acid** or **alkaline** the soil is. Soil pH is important because it impacts how well plants take up nutrients from the soil, depending on the plant species. Some species of plants take up nutrients well, regardless of pH, while others are very dependent on pH for uptake of certain kinds of nutrients. Most plants will grow well in soils with a slightly acidic pH above 5.5 and many plants will not tolerate lower acidic conditions (a lower pH number) for extended periods of time. Likewise, most plants prefer a pH below 6.5, but there are several plants that prefer neutral or slightly alkaline pH of 7.2. Some plants prefer acidic conditions, like white **pines** and plants in the ericaceous (heath) family. Other plants, like many kinds of fruit trees, can tolerate much higher pH's above 6.5. Ferns and **mosses** prefer a neutral or slightly alkaline pH above 7.0. PAs may be expected to know the soil pH preference of the plants they appraise and they may be expected to know the suitability of the subject soil pH to the subject being appraised. In extreme cases, when the subject site soil requires additional maintenance to manage the soil pH, the additional maintenance will have a negative impact on the amount of care and inputs that are required. Thus, poor pH may be considered as obsolescence when calculating appraised value. When soil is suitable (no extra maintenance required), then no calculation of obsolescence is necessary. Soil pH is most reliably determined by a soil test.

Soil Nutritional Content

There are seventeen water-soluble soil nutrient compounds that are essential to plant growth. These soluble chemical compounds are most commonly identified and measured by the primary elements they contain. Plants use these nutrients in relatively large amounts or relatively small quantities. The nutrient compounds that are used in relatively large amounts are called **macronutrient**s and these chemical compounds contain nitrogen (N), phosphorus (P), potassium (K), calcium (Ca), magnesium (Mg) and sulfur (S). The nutrient compounds that are used in relatively small amounts are called **micronutrient**s (or trace elements) and these compounds contain boron (B), chlorine (Cl), manganese (Mn), iron (Fe), zinc (Zn), copper (Cu), molybdenum (Mo), nickel (Ni) and cobalt (Co). It is usually not necessary to add soil nutrients in the form of fertilizer, but some sites lack adequate amounts of elements in water-available, chemically-active forms that plants need. Some sites have levels of micronutrients that are high enough to become toxic to plants, requiring maintenance to adjust the soil nutrients to tolerant levels. In some instances, soil pH can control nutrient availability. Soil pH can have a profound impact on how well nutrients are taken up by plants.

While most soils contain enough nutrients to allow plants to complete their life cycles without the addition of fertilizers, many sites that have been altered from their natural state have significant deficiencies in nutrient availability. Croplands, urban development and residential site development are some of the more common examples of where nutrient deficiencies may be found. Plant appraisers should be familiar with the site soil nutrient characteristics and should be prepared to interpret their suitability to the species of the appraisal subject. Deficiencies in suitability that require additional fertilizer maintenance for normal plant health and growth should be considered for obsolescence as they will have a negative impact on appraised value. Soils requiring no maintenance to maintain healthy and vigorous plants are not considered nutritionally obsolete.

Organic Content

Organic matter content is another critically important soil constituent when it comes to plant life. Organic matter is the decomposing remains of plants, animals, fungi and other dead things. These decaying remains are the food source for a wide variety of soil organisms. Worms, **algae**, fungi, bacterium and many other organisms live on and around the organic components in the soil. Decaying organic substances are good at maintaining moisture in the soil and the chemically bioactive structures that soil organisms form around organic particles work to bind **soil** particles into **aggregates**. The action of soil organisms upon organic matter cultivates the soil, improves soil **porosity/permeability** and reduces soil density. This same action also causes a cascade of residual chemical activity, which converts water insoluble soil nutrients into soluble soil nutrients that plants can easily **absorb**. Even in small quantities, the organic content of the soil is a very important external characteristic of soils to plants. Most soils contain between two and ten percent organic matter. Higher amounts of organic matter, especially after organic mulch has been augmented for many years, can become a detriment to certain plants. Over-applied mulches can and do cause root/**buttress** defects and they can create super adequate concentrations of nutrients like calcium (Ca++). Soils that are lacking in organic content tend to be dryer, more prone to **erosion** and less nutritious to plants than those with higher carbon content.

The plant appraiser should be familiar with the organic content characteristics of soils and be able to understand the impact that the soil's organic characteristics will have on appraisal subject's overall health and vitality. While neither excess organic content nor deficiencies are very common, problems in organic content that necessitate increased plant maintenance may justify obsolescence reduction in appraised value. A lack of soil organic content problems requires no deduction in obsolescence.

Soil Texture

Soil texture refers to the size of the particles that make up smaller sized, insoluble soil solids. From smallest size to the largest size, soil texture is comprised of varying amounts of **clay**, **silt**, **loam** and **sand**. Clay soils tend to drain more slowly and retain water better but are typically less apt to contain larger **pore spaces**. Clay soils are denser, easily compacted (when dry) and less permeable. Some clay soils are water **impervious**. Sandy soils are typically very well drained and remain dryer than other soils. Plants growing in sandy soils usually require greater volume precipitation/irrigation events and they require them more frequently. Most plants are adapted to loamy soil conditions, but there are species specialists that have adapted to soils across the texture spectrum. (Coder)

While many plant species are adaptable to a broad range of soil textures, for some plant species, soil texture can be a challenge. PAs should be able to identify when soil's texture presents a challenge to a plant species. When a difficulty exists, the plant appraiser will be expected to credibly judge a weighted depreciation in obsolescence that is commensurate with the deficit.

Soil Bulk Density

Bulk density is most often expressed in terms of soil weight/volume in g/cm^3 but occasionally this critical soil attribute is expressed as lb/in^3. Bulk density is defined as the dry weight per unit volume of soil. Bulk density considers all the soil solids and the pore spaces that exist between the soil solids. Bulk density is the oven-dry weight of the soil material less than two millimeters in size per unit volume of soil, expressed in grams per cubic centimeter. Bulk density is critical in resource assessment modeling, such as soil **hydrology**, water budgets, leaching, nutrient-**pesticide** loading and site/species selection for transplanting landscape plants. Essentially, the higher the bulk density, the more difficulty plant roots will have growing and thriving in that soil. Plant roots will not grow in clay loam with a bulk density of 1.65 or greater. Sandy soils are more difficult to compact to root intolerable levels. (USDA, 2013)

Typically, when land improvements like **concrete** surfaces are constructed, the subsoil on which these structures are built is excavated and is well compacted before a sub-base is laid and also compacted. Proper construction methods demand that soils be compacted since compaction prevents settling of structures that are built above. Compacting the soil also prevents most types of plant roots from entering the subbase and subsoil, at least during the normal life expectancy of the structure. If the soil is not properly compacted or if time, erosion or corrosion occur, the density of the compacted soils can lessen, especially when deep penetration of water occurs repeatedly over time. Water, through the action of the soil biology of organically rich soils, can greatly reduce **soil compaction**. Likewise, a layer of mulch can encourage natural soil cultivation and can effectively reduce soil compaction.

Disturbed and manipulated soils (due to excavation) often suffer from higher bulk density conditions. Some plant species are more sensitive to densely compacted soils than others. Generally, the more sensitive a plant species is to compaction, the more important soil bulk density becomes and the less suitable the soil becomes as soil density increases. Soil bulk density is also highly dependent on soil texture. Soils with high moisture and more sand and loam tend to resist compaction quite well while dryer clay soils are more easily compacted with less effort and fewer trips across the soil surface.

The PA should be familiar with various texture characteristics of soils and be expected to understand the impact that both soil texture and soil bulk density will have on plants. The appraiser must also know the plant's soil texture preference and if that preference is affected by the soil's density. If the density of the soil has overall impact on plant health and vitality, an obsolescence reduction of value that is commensurate with the severity of the condition should be calculated and applied. A lack of bulk density problems requires no deduction in obsolescence.

Several methods are available to test the bulk density of the soil. The first method involves coring a known volume of soil, drying it completely in a vacuum, weighing the result and calculating the weight per unit volume. Another method of determining the density of the soil relative to soil moisture is with the use of a **penetrometer**, although bulk density testing and analysis is much more reliable since it does not rely on soil moisture being present.

Soil Biology

Soil biology is critically important for plant health and vitality. There are four basic groups of microorganisms that can be measured as they relate to plant health and vitality. They are fungi, bacteria, protozoa and nematodes. Each of these groups provides certain biological functions and each group can contribute to plant health. Each group also has pathogenic organisms that can infect plants and may be detrimental. Some organisms may be **symbiotic**, depending on the soil conditions.

Beneficial fungi in the soil play an important role in plant health. Soil nutrient retention, nutrient transportation, nutrient absorption, **soil structure** development and the soil structure's relationship to soil pH are soil attributes that are controlled to a great extent by fungi. The plant system of nutrient succession is directly linked to the ratio of fungi to bacteria in the soil and is the chief consideration in soil remediation. Soils lacking fungal activity have fewer resources available to benefit plants. Beneficial fungi normally exist in the soil, including the endo and ectomycorrhizal fungi that form symbiotic relationships with plant roots to form an extramatriclular root system capable of absorbing far more water and nutrients than plants without mycorrhizae. These fungi also filter out toxins and suppress pathogenic organisms in the soil. In exchange for these services, the tree supplies a steady stream of carbohydrates to the fungi. Weakened plants are less able to keep and develop these symbiotic fungi populations and may require remediation to re-establish healthy mycorrhizal populations.

Soils that lack these beneficial fungi are a very serious problem to plant health that can lead to the total breakdown of tree health and vitality. Soil fungal health can be restored by introducing fungal food resources to the soil and by introducing the mycorrhizal inoculums that are known to form beneficial associations with plants. There are several methods that can achieve this, but the most successful and least intrusive method is vertical mulching or trenching. This reduces soil compaction while creating conditions where mycorrhizal fungi can thrive. (Van Veen, 1979)

Plant appraisers should be knowledgeable about plants and the mycorrhizal fungi associations they require for health and vitality. They should also be able to recognize those conditions when mycorrhizal associations are adversely affected and what impacts those conditions will have on overall plant health and vitality. When mycorrhizal remediation is necessary to restore plant health, plant appraisers should be prepared to weigh the cause of the soil/mycorrhizal fungi deficiency and its long-term impacts on plant health and vitality. The plant appraiser should also be able to calculate obsolescence on plant value when appropriate.

The total population of soil bacteria biomass provides an indicator of abundance of food for all soil organisms, nutrient cycling capacity and general diversity of the bacterial population. The active population is the component of total biomass that is currently metabolizing oxygen; i.e., the functional fraction of the bacteria. While high bacteria and diversity are not a problem in soil biology, a high bacterium to fungi ratio points to a lack of fungal resources. That can have a series of cascading and very detrimental effects on trees. (Van Veen, 1979)

Plant appraisers may need to be able to test and analyze for soil bacteria as a matter of soil health. Judgments should be made as to any long-term health effects and whether the amount of bacterial biomass should be reflected in obsolescence of the subject.

Protozoa are typically single-celled organisms that feed upon bacteria. Flagellates and amoebae are true aerobes, meaning they must have adequate oxygen to survive, while ciliates are facultative anaerobes, meaning they can survive in low oxygen conditions. Numbers of protozoa in soil are very important as an indicator of potential nutrient cycling. If there are sufficient levels of flagellates and amoebae, then **aerobic** nutrient cycling can occur. However, high levels of ciliates can be an indicator that an aerobic nutrient cycling is occurring. (Ekelund, 1998)

Plant appraisers should be prepared to test and analyze for soil protozoans as a matter of soil/plant species health. Judgments should be made as to any long-term health effects and whether the quantity of protozoans found should be reflected in obsolescence of the subject.

Identifying and quantifying nematode constituent levels can be a very clear indicator of soil health. Nematodes provide soil nutrient cycling very similar to the protozoa. They serve a very specific function and may be categorized into several important functional groups:

Bacterial Feeders: This group of beneficial nematodes feeds on bacteria; they help to keep the bacterial populations in balance. In the process of consumption, they cycle soluble nutrients in the rhizosphere of the fine roots of trees.

Fungal Feeders: As the name would suggest, this group of nematodes feeds on fungi, again, keeping fungi populations in balance and cycling nutrients in the root zone. Many of these types of nematodes also feed on fungi that can cause disease in plants. Having a good population and variety of these organisms can be an asset for plants that are more susceptible to some types of fungal diseases are grown.

Predatory Nematodes: These nematodes are specialists in eating other nematodes Typically, they prey on root feeding-nematodes and can help minimize their ability to cause damage. This group will also consume protozoa and some types of micro-arthropods. This preditory feeding becomes an excellent source of nutrients for plants.

Fungal/Root Feeders: This is an interesting group of nematodes. They typically act as fungal feeders, but if the population of fungi is low or if the right combination of plant and nematode are present, they will eat the roots of the plants. This group is an indicator for both healthy fungal populations and, at the same time, for potential disease issues in the plants.

Root Feeders: This group of nematodes is parasitic to plants. There is a wide variety of these types and, depending on the genus and the plant being grown, can be a real problem for plant health. The loss of as few as one feeder root per gram of soil can hinder plant productivity. This group of nematodes is an indicator of soil health.

By looking at the total population of nematodes, examining levels of functional groups and cross-referencing to the plant species, a fairly good picture of soil productivity can be developed. (Goodey, 1963)

Plant appraisers should be familiar with the different groups of nematodes and should be capable of testing their presence and populations. Judgments may need to be made as to whether or not the various levels of nematodes are relevant to the appraisal assignment and whether or not obsolescence should be credibly applied.

While soil samples may be tested and analyzed for soil organism health in detail, that depth of investigation is not usually included in the initial plant appraisal scope of work. If it is clear that an adverse soil health condition exists and that the condition requires a thorough examination of the soil biology, then a discussion of expanding the scope of work with the client may be warranted. Once the soil biology is known, the appraiser may judge the relevant facts for obsolescence.

Pollution/Pesticide Tolerance

Sometimes, for various reasons, plant exposures to known pollutants and/or pesticides is a certainty. Some plant species are quite tolerant of pollution/pesticides while others are quite susceptible to injury due to exposure to pesticides/pollutants. Pollutant and pesticide exposures are often capable of weakening plants, making them more susceptible to pest problems or exacerbating other external conditions that are not ideal for the plant. Pollution and pesticides have the effect of lowering a plant's overall health, vigor and vitality. Plant appraisers need to know which pollutants/pesticides may be of concern, which species of plant are susceptible to damage and what the visual/health effects of exposure will be on subject plants. Plant appraisers should be capable of assessing and calculating a weighted deduction for obsolescence when pollution/pesticide exposure has occurred or when there is a certainty that such will occur in the future.

Many plants are tolerant of pollutants and are quite good at removing pollution from the air. This **ecosystem** service can be calculated as a functional benefit of trees when that ecosystem service value is sought as a benefit.

CHAPTER FOUR

Identification of Plant Species Physical Characteristics

It has been 140 years since Margaret Wolfe Hungerford penned those famous words "Beauty is in the eye of the beholder," yet those profound words still ring true today. However difficult to quantify, beauty is one of the intangible but desirable benefits that plants can produce. People can and do go to great expense and efforts to obtain beauty in their landscapes. While many people consider landscape beauty to be ephemeral and quite difficult to quantify (or at the very least they consider beauty to be subjective), educated and experienced landscape and plant professionals have a more noble insight into this area of often-misunderstood expertise. An authority on landscape beauty can describe, in detail, those attributes and characteristics that make a garden beautiful and what makes it desirable to owners or even to potential buyers and sellers. Authorities on landscape design can also give a detailed account of landscape beauty in terms of scarcity. While beauty may be in the eye of the beholder to the uninitiated, professionals are among the more discerning. Professionals follow certain guidelines in creating beauty in the landscape. There are many landscapes, but relatively few are truly beautiful to behold. A landscape of exceptional beauty is rare indeed.

There have been many efforts to quantify the wide and varied tangible and intangible benefits that owners enjoy by being surrounded with beautiful landscaping. Even so, the task of quantifying landscaping is very difficult from a real estate market perspective. It is difficult, if not impossible, to discern and quantify the anticipated, intangible landscape benefits (like the sense of well-being and joy one anticipates while walking through a beautiful garden) in terms of an easy-to-calculate formula. The amount of worth representing the landscape contribution to **market** value of a whole property is not easily or simply discerned.

The reason for this is simple. Real estate appraisers have done an admirable job of capturing, quantifying and compiling many of the characteristics data that are typically used for residential and commercial real estate financial instruments. REAs are very good at analyzing and processing those characteristics that are required and relevant to mortgage lending and borrowing. Conversely, the real estate appraisal community has completely ignored landscaping elements of value in these efforts. Opinions about landscape value require a more sophisticated and detailed knowledge of plant species, landscape design, and in-use benefits that trees and landscaping produce. Plant appraisal also requires an understanding of how trees are measured for size and how they are analyzed for physical conditions. What is needed, when it comes to the appraisal of trees and plants, is a thorough examination of the specific characteristics that are relevant to the benefits that landscapes produce.

Detailed in this book, you will find the most relevant plant and site characteristic descriptions, the roles that these characteristics play in ornamental landscaping and their relevance in plant appraisal principles and procedures. It is the intangible benefits that are produced by a plant's aesthetic characteristics that this segment of the *Professional Amenity Plant Appraisal Handbook* examines. While not exhaustive, this segment gives a clear understanding of what the main plant aesthetic characteristics are, why those characteristics are desirable and how to evaluate the aesthetic characteristics in the plant appraisal process.

The importance of landscape aesthetics to property owners is universally underestimated by real estate appraisers who lack the specialized knowledge and skill in these critical areas: plant characteristics, the functional benefits they produce, intangible benefits they produce and the underlying principles that make well executed landscape architectural design desirable. To understand what makes landscape plants desirable, we must first look to those plant characteristics that contribute aesthetically to the landscape as they are perceived by owners.

Leaf Persistence

Landscape aesthetics are dynamic. Shadows cast by a tree canopy change as the sun moves along its course throughout the day. Accent lighting at night provides another unique aesthetic altogether. Seasons change throughout the year, and the appearance of landscape plants will exhibit seasonal characteristics in due time. **Leaf** persistence is a critically important characteristic. All plants lose their old leaves every twelve to eighteen months. **Evergreen** plants display green leaves throughout the winter. These plants hold onto their green leaves as their new leaves develop in **spring**. When spring leaves are fully developed, the older evergreen leaves change color and fall off. Other plants have leaves that change color in the fall and drop off, leaving the twigs barren of **foliage** until spring. Well-placed plants that have either persistent foliage or seasonal persistence can add greatly to the aesthetics of landscape design.

The trees and the water features set the stage for a sculptural focal point. The potent landscape lighting introduces another dynamic element to the design that would otherwise not exist. In this sculpture, the nightly illumination brings to light new aspects of the sculpture that would otherwise be unseen.

Plant appraisers should be familiar with the persistence of leaves and be aware of any unusual or extra maintenance and care that may be needed because of a landscape design that poorly anticipates leaf or twig drop. Also, some trees tend to drop leaves and litter throughout the year while others are more seasonally oriented. Unusual messiness of a tree in a high traffic site costs more to maintain and extreme messiness may justify a deduction in obsolescence. Cleaner trees with a more seasonal orientation are less costly to maintain and do not justify a deduction.

In landscape design, seasonal color and rhythmic leaf drop can provide an important dynamic aesthetic. When well designed, this dynamic in aesthetics can be very desirable. Likewise, landscapes that have an evergreen plant growing where a **deciduous** plant should have been placed (and vice versa) can be a significant detriment to the desirable aesthetic. When a deficiency in design is clear, the plant appraiser may make a weighted obsolescence deduction in value based on poor species placement obsolescence of the persistence characteristic.

Growth Habit

This broad categorization is characteristic of the general shape and ultimate size that plants can reach. Each species of plant has growth character tendencies or habits that will vary somewhat depending on the site conditions. Some plants have stronger tendencies toward growth habit than do others. The growth habit, size and shape that a plant develops in its native habitat is considered to be its dominant habit form. While some plant species are capable of easily adapting to a broad range of site conditions and spaces that fall outside of their native habitat, other species (like palms) have limited habit forms that closely match their native habitat.

As an example, trees growing in a forest environment tend to grow tall, slender trunks that allow their canopies to compete for more sunlight near the top of a dense forest canopy. These trees are protected from wind by surrounding trees and the result is that they have less developed undergirding soil/root support. In developed sites where forests are removed and some of the forest trees are retained, exposed trees are more prone to sun scalding of the trunks and tall, exposed canopies are more prone to wind throw.

Conversely, trees growing singly or as specimens in locations where they are not shaded tend to grow short, broad canopies. Trees growing in wide open spaces are exposed to the forces of wind and this causes their trunks to develop greater taper with greater amounts of wood. They also develop larger and more robust buttresses and buttress roots.

Plant appraisers should be familiar with the varying growth tendencies and habits of plants and should be familiar with the site conditions where a plant is growing. The plant appraiser may be called upon to judge if the growth habit of the plant is appropriate for the site conditions and they should be able to determine if there are deficiencies in regard to growth habit. Where deficiencies exist, the appraiser may need to calculate the weighted obsolescence of the deficiency in growth habit.

Inflorescence

Flowers are an ephemeral characteristic in plants. Some plant species are showy and offer fantastic seasonal display while others have inconspicuous flowers and offer no aesthetic benefit at all. Oftentimes, in landscape architectural design, floral plants are selected and planted en masse to achieve a desirable seasonal color effect. A good example would be when the azaleas bloom during the Masters Golf Tournament at Augusta National Golf Club in Augusta, Georgia.

Inflorescence Color

Color of the inflorescence should be appropriate for the landscape theme and for how well the plant's color achieves the desired landscape effect. The plant appraiser should be able to recognize what the desired landscape effect is and how well the subject plant is able to generate the desired effect, and be able to identify any deficiencies. If warranted, the plant appraiser may assess any appropriately weighted obsolescence in the appraisal calculation for deficiencies.

Inflorescence Showiness

The showiness in plant **inflorescence** is the adequacy or inadequacy of a plant's flowers to achieve a desired effect on the landscape user. The plant's inflorescence should be showy enough to achieve the desired landscape effect. The plant appraiser should be able to recognize what the desired effect is and how well the subject plant is able to meet the need. If warranted, the plant appraiser may assess any appropriately weighted obsolescence in the appraisal calculation for the deficiency.

This display of inflorescence is particularly showy because the tree blooms in early spring before the leaves of other deciduous trees have developed fully and it produces many colorful flowers.

Inflorescence Time of Year

Landscape design **plant selections** are theme-based and effect-based. Since flowers of plants tend to bloom seasonally, the design's architect makes selections that are seasonally appropriate to achieve a desirable effect. Sometimes this desirable effect is creating interest throughout the year and sometimes it is creating interest at a certain time of year. The plant selection for floral color timing should be appropriate to the theme and the intended purpose of the design. Plant appraisers may need to be aware of the species' timing of inflorescence and if the timing is appropriate for the intended desirable landscape effect. If there are elements of inflorescence timing that are inappropriate or are distracting to the intended effect, the appraiser may apply any appropriately weighted obsolescence in the appraisal calculation. Be aware that any judgments of depreciation should be defensible, and the appraiser should be able to articulate why a deduction was necessary in the appraisal process.

The bark of this paperbark maple tree has interesting texture, brilliant color and is a showy contrast to the light-colored flowers and other plants in the background.

Leaf/Fruit/Bark

While inflorescence is a leading factor of plant selection in landscape design, other plant characteristics are often used in conjunction with inflorescence to create desirable landscape effects throughout the year. These characteristics include leaves, fruit and **bark**. Leaves can produce changes in color as they first emerge from buds, and mature to a different color in late spring and summer. Leaves can display a different range of colors in the fall. Of all plant parts, leaves have the greatest ability to create seasonal color and texture impacts.

Leaf/Fruit/Bark Seasonality

Seasonal color and leaf drop can provide an important dynamic aesthetic in landscape design. When well designed, this dynamic aesthetic can be very desirable. Seasonal absence of leaves coincides with bark displays after leaf fall. When bark is showy, the display changes the character of the landscape and this effect can be very desirable when properly executed.

Some plants display seasonal interest all year long while others change very little throughout the year. Depending on the landscape element and the desired effect, seasonality of plants may be either desirable or undesirable. For example, specimen or accent plants usually have some sort of seasonal

Shrubs with showy bark display seasonal interest in winter.

display that complements other plants in a landscape feature or element. Foundation plantings near a building, however, are selected because they do not change much throughout the year.

Deficiencies exist when the desired landscape seasonal effect is inadequately achieved. When a deficiency in landscape design is clear, the plant appraiser may make a weighted obsolescence deduction in value based on poor placement or the lack of presence in the seasonal display characteristics.

Leaf/Fruit/Bark Color

The display of color is very important in landscape design, perhaps the most important of all landscape design elements. The color of flowers, leaves, fruit and bark all contribute to the character of the subject plant. These colors are determined by the landscape architect's selection of plants in the development of the design-themed elements and in the overall purpose of the design. As the differing characteristics of the subject plant contribute color to the landscape design at different times, the subject's contribution to the design element can evoke a desirable response in the user of the landscape garden.

Plant appraisers should be aware of the seasonal colors that a plant species produces and should be prepared to ascertain their importance to the landscape design. If the plant selection is poor or limiting to the desired and intended effect of the landscape element or if color is distracting

The color of these Japanese maple leaves produces a sharp contrast to other trees and the sky beyond.

Some plants offer colorful fruit that inspires seasonal interest.

to the design as a whole, the appraiser may justify an obsolescence deduction for color in the appraisal process.

Leaf/Fruit/Bark Texture

Texture is another dynamic element of deciduous plants. As spring approaches, barren twigs and **limbs** of deciduous trees and shrubs transform into lush, shade-producing canopies that can vary considerably from species to species in color and texture. As leaves grow to full size, the textures displayed in the canopy of plants morph into summertime, casting shade and reflecting sunlight until the cooler days of fall trigger yet another transformation of colors and textures. These seasonal changes can provide landscape architects with a wide and varied pallet of seasonally triggered textures.

Evergreens offer their own special characteristics of texture but are not as subject to changes by the season as are their deciduous counterparts. Evergreens come in a wide array of textures, from fine-needled specimens to broadleaved trees and shrubs. When the texture of plants is appropriate to the intended effect in the design, no deductions for obsolescence are necessary, but if there is a clear deficiency in texture, obsolescence for the deficiency may be applied.

Leaf/Fruit/Bark Size/Shape

Plant foliage comes in all manner, shapes and sizes. Landscape architects select plants for their potential to display this characteristic in order to achieve an effect that supports the landscape design theme and purpose. While important, leaf shape and size are usually subordinate to other plant aesthetic characteristics, such as texture and color. Plant appraisers should be aware of a plant's leaf size and shape and how it affects the plant's other aesthetic characteristics. Occasionally, this characteristic may be detrimental to the overall design theme or purpose and may be cause for an obsolescence deduction in the plant appraisal process, especially if more suitable cultivars exist that are better suited for achieving the desirable effect.

Leaf/Fruit/Bark Luster/Sheen

Luster and sheen refer to the qualities of light that are reflected off the surface of leaves. Glossy leaves have a very smooth surface and have a shiny, reflective quality upon which polarized skylight will create points of glare from a subject's canopy. Plants with rough surface reflect only diffused non-polarized light and they do not project small points of glare from the subject. While this characteristic is important from an architectural design standpoint, luster and sheen are usually subordinate to other plant aesthetic characteristics. Occasionally, this characteristic may be detrimental to the overall design theme or purpose and may be cause for an obsolescence deduction in the plant appraisal process, especially if more suitable cultivars exist that are better suited for achieving the desirable effect, either with or without luster/sheen. This is especially true where the luster and sheen of a plant is affected by physical deterioration due to insects or disease activity. A good example would be Chinese Holly *(Ilex cornuta)* that is badly infested with scale insects and the luster of the leaves is obscured by sooty mold.

CHAPTER FIVE

Identification of Physical Deterioration Characteristics

Physical deterioration of plant parts will be caused by a myriad of things. This data identifies deterioration of the physical plant parts regardless of cause. This information will be used to analyze how well a plant is able to deliver benefits to users based on the limitations imposed by the physical deterioration of each individual plant part. Also, specific plant parts are responsible for delivering specific benefits to users, so the appraiser will need to look at the plant part, the benefits that part delivers and the obsolescence that the plant part's physical condition/deterioration imposes on delivery of those benefits.

The anatomical structures of plants are the points from which the discernable benefits of plants are delivered. Each plant part represents a specific benefit delivery point. For example, the entire canopy of the tree delivers shade and leaf color benefits, but the canopy is the sum of each leaf as each leaf delivers its portion of the benefit. If the condition of the benefit producing part of the tree is less than perfect (due to physical damage or deterioration), the plant value is is diminished in its diminished ability to produce that benefit. This is the essence of physical deterioration as it applies to plant value. Obsolescence of physical condition occurs in the delivery of benefits that are delivered by specific plant parts, but obsolescence does not occur in plant parts that do not deliver the specific benefit being depreciated.

Since plants regenerate over time, the severity of deterioration may be broken down into two categories, extent and permanence. The extent of deterioration is related to the overall conditions of the various plant parts. Damage to all leaves of a tree's canopy is more severe than damage to the leaves of a branch or limb. The permanence of deterioration to tree parts may be categorized by duration. Damage that will repair itself in a short period of time may mean only a temporary loss of benefits will be expected, while irreparable damage may mean a long term or permanent loss of benefits that are produced. The plant appraiser will have to determine the cause and extent of deterioration in order to calculate internal deterioration obsolescence. Depending on the scope of work of the assignment, calculating deterioration may involve testing and analysis of the soil, tree structure and evaluation of plant health and use. Physical deterioration analysis may also involve performing tree risk analysis. If remedial treatments will be needed to repair or restore a tree/site to health, treatment recommendations/costs may also become part of the appraisal assignment scope of work.

Roots

Since the roots of plants are most always underground, their ability to deliver desirable aesthetic benefits are very limited. Occasionally, when roots are intended for use as food or habitat, they may serve to provide aesthetics in a very limited role. Functionally, roots fulfill many important roles in the structure and health of trees and plants. Roots absorb water and nutrients and they stabilize the soil while anchoring the plant to the earth. They are important in vegetative reproduction and they compete for soil resources among other plants. Roots are very important in soil stabilization and in supporting other plant parts in the overall health and structure of the plant. Sometimes, when roots are exposed near the soil surface, they add an aesthetic benefit.

Most of the root system of this crape myrtle tree have no aesthetic value since they cannot be seen. The roots do serve many functional uses and provide a variety of benefits that may have great worth.

Trunk/Bark

The trunk or main stem is important in support and is critical in supplying vertical elevation of trees. Depending on tree species, trunk bark changes as a tree matures. The plates and the fissures between the plates often gain a statelier appearance as tree trunk size increases. Also, the color of bark can change with age, giving older trees a more distinguished appeal. Trunk bark is also a protector of the living tree cells and wood that exist below the bark. Trunk injuries can allow decay fungi, insects and other diseases to invade a tree, resulting in structural deterioration, or they can be merely cosmetic and add to the desirable character of the tree. There are other structural defects, such as leans, sweeps and bows, that can have a negative impact on structural soundness, but they can also add to the aesthetic appeal of a tree trunk. Defects can also make trees less safe than they ought to be. Care for safety should be taken into account when evaluating the aesthetic defect as a benefit.

The trunk of this tree has a large hollow that has decayed over many years. The buttress was excavated to check the structural integrity of the buttress and roots.

The fatal car crash at this site also caused significant impact and fire injury to this tree trunk. Since tree trunks are less redundant than any other tree part, injuries can have a much more severe impact on the opinion of tree value.

Positive indicators (fungal conks) like this Ganoderma sp. are sure signs that the trunk of this willow tree has been aggressively dissolved for some time; it is a sure sign that this trunk will fail in the near future.

The lean of this tree, combined with defects in the tree's root structure, made this tree too dangerous to keep. The only option for mitigating the risk was removal. While this tree could not be reasonably mitigated due to the risks involved, many trees have unusual character and growth habits that make them aesthetically more valuable. Care must be taken to weigh potential risks when evaluating tree defects for their aesthetic value.

Scaffold Branches/Bark

Scaffold branches serve a similar function as tree trunks, although they should be smaller, younger and more numerous. Scaffold branches support smaller branches and the other structures attached to them. While a tree's trunk has a predominantly vertical orientation, depending on species and site conditions, scaffold branches usually take on a more horizontal orientation. Because of this, leans, sweeps and bows can be perfectly normal for scaffold branches. Like the trunk, though, branch bark is important to branch health and the prevention of decay fungi. Any wound in a branch can be a cause for calculating physical deterioration when the benefits of the scaffold branch are diminished. As with all larger tree parts, safety should be considered when evaluating tree defects.

Scaffold branch structure is more redundant than trunk. The bark character and physical conditions are both important to aesthetic and functional benefits.

Branches/Limbs/Twigs

Branches limbs and twigs support the leafy canopy. These structures are smaller still from trunks and scaffold branches and their orientation is more a function of their location within the canopy. Trees often self-prune and detach inner canopy twigs and smaller branches. While scaffold branches are a scarce but, more or less, permanent fixture in trees, the branches,

While twigs and branches are important support structures for leaves, buds and flowers, they do not contribute directly to the delivery of functional and aesthetic benefits as significantly as do other more prominent plant parts. Dead twigs are an indication of obsolescence.

twigs, limbs and structures attached to them are highly redundant. This makes these smaller features more expendable. Sometimes deficiencies in branch structure are similar among all canopy elements and sometimes deficiencies are limited to only a small portion of a canopy. Typically, small branches are not deducted for both health and structural integrity. Larger branches are graded for both health and structure and included safety considerations. Either way, the specific benefits that are delivered by branches, limbs and twigs may be diminished by their physical condition.

Buds/Leaves/Flowers/Fruits

This is the point where most of the aesthetic and functional benefits are delivered by plants. While other parts of the plant can deliver some aesthetic benefits, they pale in comparison to the leaves, flowers, buds and fruit. Leaves and flowers are the most visually interesting, most colorful and most seasonally dynamic parts of trees. Leaves, flowers, buds and fruit are critical to plant health and beauty, but they are not a structurally important plant element. Leaves, flowers, buds and fruit are also the most redundant parts of plants. Deficiencies in the delivery of benefits by leaves may be limited to a small portion of the canopy or they may be widespread throughout the entire canopy. Physical obsolescence of buds, leaves and flowers are determined by the leaf, flower or bud conditions that limit their delivery of potential benefits. The inability to deliver the benefits (due to physical deterioration) is the essence of assessing physical deterioration in buds, leaves, flowers and fruit.

Leaves are a plant's primary means of delivering plant benefits. Here, fall color is displayed in spectacular fashion.

CHAPTER SIX

Identification of Functional Benefits Characteristics

THE FUNCTIONAL BENEFITS OF PLANTS AND TREES ARE THE quantitative landscape user deliverables that will be analyzed for efficiency (obsolescence) by the appraiser. They are limited by various things such as poor landscape architectural design placement and plant species/site selection and/or deficiency in physical deterioration.

GPA9 has a basic list of suggested **functional goals** and aesthetic benefits beginning on page 53. This list is a good starting point in the preliminary examination of the benefits that plants can produce, but it is by no means an exhaustive one. In this chapter, I will describe some of the various functional tree and plant benefits in detail and show how those benefits are applicable to professional plant appraisal. While some of the benefits that plants produce are exclusive to an owner, (such as the fruit a tree produces that may be harvested) some of the benefits trees provide may go to the owner and to others beyond the owner's property boundary (like shade that is cast upon an owner and their neighbor).

Environmental Services Contribution Ratings

A well-maintained and park-like appearance, as well as other specific characteristics, may significantly enhance the ornamental and aesthetic contribution of trees. Of all the potential uses that trees can contribute to an owner's landscape, the environmental service contributions are the least subjective and most closely relevant as a measure of cost. This is because many of the functional environmental benefits that trees produce can be created through means other than plants. For example, trees that provide shade for cattle production can be replaced by a wood or metal structure that casts the same amount of shade as the subject tree. The cost to build and implement a shade-providing structure is an elementary calculation of construction and maintenance. Some environmental benefits may have a cost equivalency, such as oxygen generation, but may have no credible market equivalency. It is the quantitative nature of functional characteristics that makes the measurability of benefits less subjective and thereby less subject to artistic interpretation or preference.

While many of the aesthetic qualities and costs of plants are rooted in the subjective interpretation of plant use, those aesthetic uses are nonetheless meaningful in plant appraisal problems. One can easily measure the cooling effect of trees by calculating the amount of radiation that they block but estimating how well the texture of a foundation plant accentuates a building cannot be so easily tied to a dollar figure. Anyone who has been in a car in an unshaded parking space on a hot, sunny summer day can tell you that the temperature inside a car can rise to deadly potential. People instinctively know that parking in the shade on a hot, sunny day dramatically reduces temperatures. You can easily measure this effect with a thermometer. There are many functional **ecosystem services** that trees provide and these can be measured, quantified and produced at a cost. In the calculation of benefits, form is subordinate to function.

Vegetation Control

Reducing sunlight is an excellent means of controlling many types of understory growth. Most plant seeds have the potential to grow to maturity but very few reach that potential where mature trees already exist. Many seeds germinate over time and typically there are a great many seedlings in ratio to a single mature tree. The reason that seedlings do not reach maturity where mature trees exist is primarily because the mature canopy trees filter out photosynthesizing electromagnetic wavelengths of sunlight. Understory plants essentially starve for lack of enough sunlight. The mature tree canopy has the same effect on all sun-loving plant species; thus, a mature, dense canopy is an excellent and natural way to control many types of vegetation. The only types of vegetation that can grow under a mature, dense tree canopy are those that are adapted to low light or heavy shade conditions. These types of plants are almost always small, slow growing and are prone to damage from excessive sunlight and higher temperatures.

As a stand of trees reaches maturity (where the tree canopies coalesce to form a solid umbrella of canopy shade), equilibrium is reached where undergrowth is controlled simply by the shade tree canopy cover. If canopy shade trees are damaged, a greater amount of photosynthetic light reaches the **ground** and new varieties of vegetative growth will immediately began to appear from dormant seeds. The masses of new growth will require routine control measures to avoid understory from becoming impassable with overgrowth. A loss of canopy will necessarily increase the amount of sunlight reaching the ground and the entire **ecology** of a site may become changed for the worse, restricting certain types of use, such as walking or viewing **wildlife**. There have been many instances where the loss of canopy and the resulting overgrowth has disrupted vistas.

Wildlife Habitat

The structure and composition of a site will change over time in a process called succession. A grassy field or clear-cut site will eventually become an old-growth forest given enough time. Certain wildlife will be favored at a site as different successional changes occur. For example, early-successional stages may have more fruit/seeds for small birds, while an increase in vertical space occurs as trees grow taller and larger, encouraging small animals to thrive. Larger mature trees often develop a cavity and that will attract late-successional wildlife where some larger animals live. Depending on the type of management that is employed, a successional ecological stage can be either maintained or altered to provide habitat for different successional groups of wildlife. (Morrison M., 2006)

Wildlife habitat is an important public use of amenity trees. Enjoying wildlife is an important benefit to people that can have great value due to the enormous costs of replacing wildlife habitats.

To enhance the vertical structure of a site, it is important to keep understory and mid-story vegetation intact. Since wildlife species usually specialize on particular layers of site ecology, management depends on developing ideal components for foraging or for nesting. Although removing shrubs and saplings creates an open, park-like aesthetic, it will prohibit some understory-dependent plant and animal species from using a site. Overstory trees are used by a variety of birds for foraging and/or nesting. Some tree foliage is critically important in attracting desirable insects, like certain cherished butterflies and moths.

Tree cavities provide shelter, den and nest sites for many wildlife species, but these same cavities can also be indicators of tree safety problems in high-use sites. Trees with cavities should be professionally evaluated if they exist where compromised structural integrity can be a threat to people or property, such as those near campsites. An expert tree **risk** assessor can recommend actions that will minimize risks to an acceptable level.

When wildlife habitat is a relevant characteristic and benefit, it is crucial for the PA to know how a site's wildlife diversity may be affected by

This enormous four-foot diameter cherrybark oak (Quercus pagoda) was taken in an illegal timber harvest from an apex wildlife refuge site. The trees of this site had been growing for nearly 100 years and it would take at least half that long for the habitat to be restored to the apex level.

The canopies of the trees create vertical structure in this apex habitat. The canopy serves to suppress understory plants and the fruit of the trees supports larger mammals and birds of prey. The wildlife-viewing platform in the lower left portion of the photo is almost indistinguishable from the remainder of the site.

alteration of the ecosystem. Familiarity with the broad and/or vertical structure habitats and early to late-successional habitats are very helpful. If there has been damage done to the habitat of certain wildlife, such that wildlife can no longer be enjoyed or is significantly diminished, the cost to restore the wildlife site to its pre-damaged condition may be a measure of value. The PA may need to be educated on the restoration techniques and the costs to perform them. Even if smaller trees can be planted to improve the vertical structure of the wildlife habitat near to its pre-damaged conditions, it may take years of sustained maintenance effort to reach an effective level of succession.

Noise Attenuation

According to the National Arbor Day Foundation, trees can have a dampening effect on noise pollution. For example, a tree buffer of sufficient height and depth can significantly reduce road noise. Several factors can influence the effectiveness trees have as a means of noise attenuation.

The first factor that contributes to the effectiveness of a tree noise buffer is the density of the trees' foliage. The second is the persistence of their foliage and, third, the size of the noise buffer. A 150-foot buffer of evergreen trees is needed to reduce car noise from 80 dBs to 65 dBs. That is the difference between the noise level experienced at 50 feet from a diesel truck rolling down a highway at 50 mph and the background noise level experienced in a large business office.

If noise attenuation is a relevant characteristic of the appraisal problem, it will be important to assess the effectiveness of the tree buffer against sources of noise pollution. In damage cases, it may be necessary to establish the effectiveness of the buffer before the damage compared to the effectiveness of noise dampening after the damage. For example, a reduction of noise that is less than 3 decibels is not perceptible by humans. As with other restorative efforts, it may take smaller trees a long time to create the pre-damaged noise dampening effects. To provide a fully adequate buffer to reduce the total volume of noise, trees are strategically located. To diffuse, reflect, alter and reduce noise levels, the dampening and buffering of noise is mostly dependent on the presence of plant foliage, but the woody tissue of trees and plants does play an important role in lowering the frequency of noise. The PA may be expected to be capable of measuring noise levels and/or frequencies and they should be familiar with the planting techniques that are employed to mitigate noise pollution when noise attenuation is a relevant characteristic.

This tree buffer provides screening and effective noise attenuation to the development above from the busy highway below. The trees of this site also offer seasonal interest to both motorists and homeowners.

Cooling

Trees can provide radiant heat shelter and **transpirational cooling** benefits to wildlife and to habitable structures. Mature deciduous trees can save up to 30% in the costs of cooling a structure. Tree leaves accomplish cooling by reflecting radiant light and heat from the sun. Trees **absorb** soil water, converting it into atmospheric water vapor through evapotranspiration. Because of their unique characteristics, trees can reduce air temperatures by as much as 20 degrees during the day. This translates into suitable wildlife habitat that would otherwise not be available and it creates a greater variety of potential land uses by people.

The transpirational cooling that trees produce provides habitat for wildlife.

If trees provide a significant amount of daytime cooling, the cooling effects may be perceived as a functional benefit. As a restorative measure, planting new trees and allowing them to reach maturity over time will replace cooling effects of the trees that are lost. It is important for the PAs to consider the condition of trees and how that condition might affect a tree's cooling abilities when cooling is a relevant characteristic. It may also be important to consider what restorative efforts might be imposed to re-establish those same effects when they are lost.

There are several types of information that may be helpful in credibly establishing the cooling benefits of trees. Cooling can be measured by taking temperature readings in the shade of a tree and readings in direct sunlight. One direct indicator of the cooling benefit that a tree produces is the change in utility consumption when a tree casts shade compared to the consumption without the benefit of tree shade. This consumption comes with a cost and it is possible to calculate a value based on additional energy consumption due to lack of shade. Another approach to value is to calculate the cost to produce the tree shade.

Light Shield

The canopies of trees can, under the right circumstances, provide desirable shielding from sun glare at different times of day or at different times of year. This tangible functional effect can be partial or total depending on the species of plant and how it is placed for use as a light shield. Typically, the amount of shielding is denoted in terms of hours per day or hours per year. Photometers may also be used to directly quantify the amount of shielding that a tree produces at a given time.

Deciduous plants can provide shielding during certain daylight hours in spring, summer and fall when leaves are present and less when leaves are not present. Evergreen trees provide shielding throughout the year during the daylight hours when light is a problem. Also, the effects of the sun's ultraviolet rays can be destructive to the surfaces of many man-made materials. The light-shielding qualities of trees can extend the service life of many things like asphalt, vinyl siding and paint.

Costs to produce sunlight shielding can be calculated in several ways, but the most common and relevant way to calculate light shield production costs is to transplant suitable size and species of flora to produce the desired effect. Light-shielding structures may also be constructed and the cost to build them calculated.

Plant appraisers should be aware of situations when light shielding is a benefit to plant owners and be able to form opinions about how and when subject plants are used as light shields. The PA may be called upon to judge the effectiveness of a plant's light shielding abilities as intended in regard to the site's architectural design, species selection and the plant's placement. The appraiser should be able to articulate the importance of this benefit in the appraisal process. Where there are clear deficiencies, such as poor species selection at a site that clearly calls for designed light shielding with plants, the PA may apply a weighted deduction for obsolescence in the appraisal process.

Erosion Control

Plants must grow in soil to live and thrive, but soils also benefit from tree **root** development. Trees and other plants create water-insoluble, soil-penetrating roots that are capable of binding and aggregating the soil. They also develop symbiotic relationships with other soil organisms. This binding and aggregation of soil particulate by a root system's extramatricular mycorrhizal fungi mantles and fungal hyphae prevents erosion of the soil.

Together, these fungal-root matrices form a complex water insoluble network that is essentially a three-dimensional fabric that is highly resistant to the effects of water and wind erosion. This fungal fabric permits water and dissolved minerals to percolate and infiltrate the soil matrix to reduce water runoff while simultaneously preventing soil particulate from eroding away.

Excavated sites that are even mildly sloped and where soils have been manipulated lack these plant-produced structures. Depending on the type, soil may be highly susceptible to erosion without them. Although roots and fungi are quite water insoluble, dead roots and fungi are not at all resistant to the effects of being dissolved by fungal decay. Dead roots and fungi usually decay and dissolve rapidly after plants have died.

The loss of vegetation on a site will cause a twofold effect on soil stability. First, plants that do not exist can no longer produce enough carbohydrate to form the mycorrhizal symbiosis and the plants themselves will no longer be able to create soil-penetrating roots. The result is that preexisting root-fungal structures decompose and the soil loses its ability to resist erosion. Within a few years, decay of the roots may become extensive enough that water erosion may become a threat to soil stability where plants were once located. Oftentimes, when plants are lost due to excavation, remedial action must be taken to prevent erosion. Growing new, suitable plants can prevent erosion from becoming a problem. There are also silt fences and other structures that can be constructed at costs to reduce or eliminate erosion.

The plant appraiser may be called upon to recognize when soil erosion is a risk and when remedial action is necessary to minimize the threat. Plant appraisers must also be able to recognize the benefits that plants provide in preventing soil erosions and be capable of judging how effectively plants provide this benefit. When vegetation is intentionally planted by design to prevent erosion, the plant selected for the purpose may vary in its ability to perform the task. When a deficiency in designed plant selection for erosion control effectiveness is clear, then the plant appraiser may (when warranted) apply a weighted deduction for obsolescence in the appraisal process.

Wind Control

Trees that are planted as windbreaks reduce the quantity of dust and odor that is picked up by wind. Trees and shrubs clean the air of particles of all sizes by interception. Interception of air pollutants may be 20 times higher in areas with trees than areas that are barren of trees. Odors and dust can become fixed to plant surfaces and can enter into the plant tissue in three ways: 1) gas diffusion through stomata; 2) on wet leaves, soluble pollutants enter through stomata in a liquid form; 3) pollutants can absorb directly into plant tissues.

Windbreak trees and shrubs absorb air pollutants when they are healthy and not under **stress**. Higher humidity can increase uptake of air pollutants into trees, which may be measured within tree canopies. Microorganisms cover plant surfaces and there is evidence that these microorganisms, which are associated with windbreak trees, also contribute to absorbing odorous chemicals and pollutants.

Windbreak trees may be referred to as pollutant air filters and trees are highly effective at physically intercepting dust, gases and microbial particles that are carried by the wind. Windbreaks reduce soil erosion that is caused by wind. In addition to air purification, trees that are planted for reducing the effects of wind can have a dramatically desirable effect on downwind landscaping and structures, protecting them from various forms of damage and protecting garden environments where presence of wind can be a problem to users.

Plant appraisers need to be aware of plants used as windbreaks and they should also be capable of describing the benefits that windbreak plants produce. When trees and shrubs are planted with the designed purpose of serving as windbreaks, the plant selected for that purpose may vary in its ability to perform the task. When a deficiency in designed plant selection for wind control effectiveness exists, the plant appraiser may (when warranted) apply a weighted deduction for obsolescence in the appraisal process.

Air Purification

Air purification benefits to consider:

- Aerosol/dust absorption
- Toxin absorption
- Odor **mitigation**
- Oxygen production
- Control wind erosion
- Protect landscape plants
- Improve land use

Carbon Sequestration

Sequestration of carbon describes a plant's ability to take in atmospheric carbon dioxide and provide for its long-term storage. The absorption and storage of carbon dioxide by plants as a means of mitigating worldwide deposition of **carbon dioxide** (CO_2) is a hotly debated and a highly politicized matter. There are some governing authorities and many people who consider the ability of plants to take carbon dioxide from the air an important benefit in mitigating atmospheric warming. The United States government spends about $100 billion annually to mitigate fossil fuel emissions. Also, utility and manufacturing industries throughout the world are concerned about carbon emissions regulations compliance. According to *Forbes* in 2011, emissions compliance standards cost the US economy $1.75 trillion. With governments, industry and individuals spending so much money on emissions each year, PAs are obliged to consider trees and plants as important players in carbon emissions mitigation and CO_2 sequestration. While carbon sequestration provides negligible benefit to individual tree owners, there are quantifiable and tangible sequestration amounts that may convert to carbon credits based on the amount of hydrocarbon containing tissues that plants produce.

Barrier

Sometimes, architectural design calls for hedges or other plants to form an impenetrable barrier that keeps people away from an area or away from part of a building. Often these barriers provide for the safety of guests or they provide security to windows or other vulnerable parts of buildings. Safety and security plantings are usually selected for their dense, impenetrable plant structure and habit, or they are selected for their thorny and/or needle-like character. Safety and security barriers are effective when they prevent people from entering an unsafe area of safety or other concern.

Plant appraisers should be familiar with the characteristic use of plants as barriers and they may be called upon to judge the effectiveness of a plant when the architecturally designed space calls for the use of plants as a barrier. Deficiencies exist when the barrier is ineffective and penetrable. When called for in the appraisal process, the appraiser may assess a weighted deduction for obsolescence.

Traffic Control

Sometimes a landscape architectural design calls for plants to be placed in such a way as to direct pedestrians or motorized traffic flow, particularly on golf courses and in parks and public spaces where people gather and move around. Plants used for this purpose are usually sturdy, robust and unusually good at taking repeated impacts from traffic or golf balls.

Plant appraisers should be familiar with the various traffic control uses of plants and they may be called upon to judge their effective use in architecturally designed spaces. Deficiencies exist when plants do not hold up to repeated traffic impacts or are placed poorly as to be confusing or cause misdirection to users. Also, keep in mind that when plants grow near vehicle traffic flows, lines of site must be maintained for safety. When warranted, the appraiser may assess a weighted deduction for obsolescence in traffic control.

Runoff Mitigation/Storm Water Management

Runoff is an important consideration as a plant appraisal characteristic because, while runoff replenishes rivers and lakes, it can also change the landscape through erosion when heavy downpours occur. Excessive rainfall can cause flooding. Flowing water is very powerful and it can cause significant changes in landscape/site terrain. Water from rushing waterways and corollary erosion can move plants. Rushing boulders and flow debris can cause significant damage to structures.

As cities develop, much of the plant canopy cover is replaced by surfaces that do not absorb water, preventing infiltration of water into the soil and accumulation of **groundwater**. The more developed and urban a site, the more storm water runoff occurs. That water must be collected by extensive systems made of curbs, storm sewers, ditches, ponds, waterways and many other forms of storm water management infrastructure. Since rainstorms cause streams to rise much more quickly in urban and residential areas, there is an increased likelihood of greater and more frequent flooding in these areas.

As water flows over the land's surface, it also picks up pollutants that include sediment, fertilizers, pesticides, animal and human waste, petroleum products, metals, salts and other chemicals. Pollution over a large land area is carried by water and is concentrated in water systems, creeks, rivers and lakes. Polluted storm water can be harmful to plants, animals and people. Runoff can carry a lot of sediment. As streams rise from precipitation, the sediment may be carried hundreds of miles and this sediment can have a dramatic, negative effect on marine life.

Municipalities and other governmental authorities are responsible for managing water runoff to prevent flooding erosion from damaging property and destroying infrastructure. Municipalities spend millions of dollars each year to ensure that drainage systems and storm water carrying infrastructure are functioning properly. One of the important ways that storm water system maintenance can be minimized and managed is by providing for large spaces of woody vegetation as **green infrastructure** that filters debris and minimizes storm water loads.

Site characteristics affecting runoff are:

- Land use
- Vegetation
- Soil type
- Drainage area
- Basin shape
- Elevation
- Slope
- Topography
- Flow orientation
- Drainage network patterns

A large portion of storm precipitation is absorbed into soils where there is significant canopy cover. Water droplets are slowed, captured

Storm water mitigation is costly in both constructing infrastructure and maintenance. Green spaces reduce storm water runoff volume, reducing costs.

and stored as groundwater, where it causes no changes to the land and where it is purified as it slowly discharges into streams through seeps and **springs**. Flooding is less frequent in these areas because much of the water runoff is slowed down, by surface duff, leaves, roots and water-absorbent organic surface matter, allowing the water to infiltrate into the spongy forest-like soils. Trees and woody plants create improved water quality, resulting in less runoff and erosion. This allows more recharging of the groundwater supply. Wooded areas also help prevent the transport of sediment and chemicals into streams, protecting many forms of aquatic life.

Plant appraisers may be called upon to recognize when trees and landscaping serve to improve soil infiltration and should be able to judge a landscape's effectiveness in preventing storm water runoff. When the landscape is designed or used for this purpose and there is a clear deficiency in the plant's abilities to perform the task, the plant appraiser should be able to assess a weighted deduction for obsolescence.

Ecological Services

While an attempt has been made to be thorough in covering the functional benefits of trees and landscaping, this list and discussion of functional benefits is by no means exhaustive. There are other relevant plant characteristics that can produce functional benefits that are not described here. PAs may explore any physical plant characteristics that provide either tangible or intangible benefits to owners, so long as:

- the benefits are described in sufficient detail that they may be reasonably perceived in use to provide valued benefits,
- the plant appraiser is qualified and capable of evaluating the effectiveness of the plant in its role of providing the benefits described,
- the plant appraiser can identify any deficiencies in that benefit role, and
- the plant appraiser can apply a weighted deduction for obsolescence in the plant appraisal process when it is warranted.

Medical Benefits

Research by Dr. Roger S. Ulrich of Texas A&M University found that visual exposure to settings with trees has produced significant recovery from stress within five minutes, as indicated by changes in blood pressure and muscle tension.

The research on trees and human health is clear. Trees help people live longer, healthier, happier lives — to the tune of ~$6.8 billion in averted health costs annually in the United States. According to a 2014 report in *Environmental Pollution*, trees directly prevented 850 deaths and 670,000 cases of acute respiratory symptoms in 2010 — the equivalent of 2.5 tons per acre of toxic air pollution removal by urban trees and forests through various biological captures.

There is ample scientific evidence to show that careful planning in design of both private and public landscape spaces can have healthful psychological effects on users and that these effects can be profoundly important, medically.

Henry David Thoreau once wrote, "I cannot preserve my health and spirits unless I spend four hours a day at least — and it is commonly more than that — sauntering through the woods and over the hills and fields, absolutely free from all worldly engagements." He knew what he was talking about. I too have often experienced the therapeutic benefits of walking in my own garden or tromping through the woods and enjoying a few minutes of solitude with my maker.

Jesus experienced this same sense of garden sanctuary during his journeys through the Promised Land. I suspect that most of us who are garden-lovers have experienced the same sensation. We are at the threshold of understanding the nature and magnitude of benefits that trees and landscaping have on human health. As we better understand these benefits, we will certainly come to better appreciate the therapeutic value of plants and landscaping.

Landscaping has known medical benefits, but many trees are also known to be allergenic pollen producers. Some allergies are more common than others and it is wise for plant appraisers to be aware of when pollen-producing trees cause or aggravate allergies and when these affects may be a liability. Tree-pollen-induced allergies in people may present the possibility of obsolescence.

Social Benefits

Research also shows that neighborhoods barren of trees and landscaping have greater crime and violence compared to their greener counterparts. Trees and landscaping produce a sense of calm and alleviate fears. Parks, greenways and landscaping attract people. People who spend their time shopping spend more money over longer periods of time when their shopping experience includes proximity to an abundance of mature trees.

Economic Benefits

Market value of real estate increases with the size and quality of professional landscaping. If you ask a REA if landscaping is important in the market value of a piece of property, they will universally tell you, "of course it is!" When you ask them how they would go about calculating it, REAs are totally lost. The reason is because the value of landscaping and trees is not parsed in the vast reservoir of available market transaction data the way that houses, driveways and other land improvements are parsed. In the conduct of real estate appraisal, detailed consideration of the landscaping, tree sizes, tree conditions and the quality of architectural placement is simply not a requirement for government-backed financial instruments like mortgages. Even though plants and landscape trees do make a difference in the behaviors of real estate market participants, real estate appraisers are typically ill-equipped to calculate those differences in behavior. In other words, when a real estate appraiser sees landscaping and trees, they see dirt, even though they either consciously or unconsciously know that trees, plants and landscaping are worth far more than dirt.

Ask the same question to real estate brokers and you will get the same kinds of answers as you would REAs. Ask the market participants (both buyers and sellers) and they will all tell you that landscaping and trees matter a great deal in the desirability and anticipation of benefits of real estate. Ask any one of these folks to quantify that desire down to dollars and cents and you will get a great disparity of answers that range wildly from market to market and from person to person within each market. The fact remains that current comparative sales data of landscaping improvements is nonexistent and that the current real estate appraisal opinions of CREMV of landscaping, plants and trees is totally subjective without deference to a cost or income analysis of those improvements.

There exists a gap between what REAs are sometimes called upon to opine and the expertise that they possess regarding amenity trees and landscaping. While amenity trees and landscaping are realty, the task of quantifying the value of trees and landscaping has traditionally been the work of educated and experienced professionals who are trained to look for clues about amenity landscape value where they actually exist — that is, in the landscape construction markets. These specialized professionals look to the industry that creates landscapes and the costs that are involved in their creation.

One of the nuances that makes landscape PAL so specialized is that, while most land improvements simply deteriorate over time and are treated with depreciation only, landscape plants and trees can appreciate over time as they grow bigger, providing more anticipated benefits. Since well-designed landscapes create more benefits (and subsequently more perceived worth) for their owners, the value of landscaping can improve over time. This increase in growth and delivery of benefits can be measured in a standardized way and converted into units of value. Comparable nursery stock and landscape construction costs can also be calculated into the same standardized units and these costs may be calculated based on the unit's production costs as landscaping. The difference in unit size, taking obsolescence of the subject into account, produces a monetary equivalent of the subject to a similar replacement new or a surrogate replacement.

Aesthetic Benefits

The famous American architect Louis Sullivan coined the phrase "form follows function" in his well-known article *The Tall Office Building Artistically Considered* in 1896. Virtually all contemporary architecture and industrial design since that time apply this principle in practice. This principle is, of course, included in all elements of landscape architectural design, as well. Since the functional benefit is always the primary goal of any landscape, it is fitting that the functional benefits of trees take precedence over the landscape's more qualitative characteristics. That is, one receives benefits of aesthetic form (characterized by the enjoyment one receives) through the quantitative experiences found in the landscape's functional uses.

In evaluating the quality of architectural landscape design, PAs always consider the functional benefits first and the aesthetic benefits are always subordinate to the functional. This forces the intangible, qualitative and subjective nature of benefits to take on the critically important quantitative basis in facts and data that are necessary for calculating a monetary equivalency in appraisal problems. It is function rather than the personal preference of the beholder's opinion about art and aesthetics that is the foundational principle in any opinion of ALSO plant value. Nevertheless, aesthetic benefits are a significant source of desirability and anticipation of benefits for plant owners and aesthetics must be considered and weighed in the appraisal process. After all, art is often the only means of communicating the intangible and/or universal things in existence, so art itself has a uniquely functional purpose with intrinsic value of its own. Some consider landscape design the most dynamic and challenging art form of all. It is also an art form that, like all glory, is perhaps more subject to atrophy than are other types of art and property.

People intuitively know when an aesthetic is good and pleasing to the eye, but I have found that they can rarely articulate aesthetics into a quantitative fashion, especially when it comes to landscape design. Most people are at a complete loss to interpret landscape aesthetics in terms of monetary value. Color, fragrance, fruit, texture, silhouette, size, shape and other characteristics may all contribute to the aesthetic character of the internal physical structures in plants, but translating that into money value opinion is challenging. The aesthetic gives value to the plant beyond its functional purposes and when designed well, the form is synergistic to the function, making the functional thing all the more desirable. That is why some wealthy people will spend $200,000 or more on an automobile. You could spend far less to get yourself from point A to point B, but I doubt that you would enjoy it nearly as much as you would driving from A to B at the controls of a brand-new Ferrari California T.

CHAPTER SEVEN

A Short Primer on Landscape Design

This portion of the text is meant to be an introductory aid to assist newcomers to professional plant appraisal in defining the most important aesthetic characteristics of plants within their architecturally designed spaces. To assist newcomers in assessing the contribution of benefits that these aesthetic characteristics might be expected to deliver. This section is by no means a comprehensive treatise on landscape architectural design and should not be construed to be an all-inclusive summary of every possible aesthetic benefit that one might perceive/receive from amenity trees and landscaping. After all, educational excellence in landscape architecture is a lifelong pursuit of which only a handful ever reach the very pinnacle. There are other relevant aesthetic characteristics, to be sure, but they fall outside the scope and effort of this handbook. I think I've covered the main topics well enough to give plant appraisers a fair run at it.

"A Short Primer on Landscape Design" is really a book within a book. Many of the folks who hope to practice professional amenity plant appraisal are woefully ill-equipped to evaluate landscape use characteristics that deliver qualitative benefits because they have never engaged in landscape design education or training and they don't have the needed experience. My thinking in placing this chapter here is to give plant appraisers some common material that will help them clearly articulate the difference between exceptionally good landscape design and exceptionally poor landscape design. My inspiration was to give a short but clear explanation of those things that make good design good and bad design bad as an aid to help professional plant appraisers do a better job of articulating both the use of landscape plants in design (the qualitative benefits that are produced) and the obsolescence that those landscape characteristics may contain. The qualitative characteristics are responsible for producing the qualitative benefits described in this "book within a book."

Plant Selection

The most challenging, time-consuming and critical step in the process of landscape design is selecting the most appropriate plant and locating it in the most appropriate place. It is this essential skill that makes good landscape architectural design good and poor design bad. Plant selection is difficult stuff and a consistently excellent caliber of plant selection is relatively rare across the vast transactions that constitute the landscaping industry. Good plant selection in design is common where competent professionals have been engaged to do the job well and poor selection in design is common where do-it-yourself and unsophisticated efforts have been used. You can almost always tell the difference when you first look. Oftentimes, to save money, do-it-yourselfers buy less expensive, poor-quality plants. Cheap, fast-growing plants are commonly available at the local big box chain store, where they are readily available to anyone that wants them. These plants are very easily transported and transplanted by anyone with a shovel, a trailer, and a pick-up truck or SUV. Professionals usually buy from reputable nurseries where the inputs to produce the right species, size and quality of plant materials makes them substantially more expensive to grow, purchase, transport and transplant.

While professional design and installation is much more expensive than amateur efforts, the value of professional work is far greater per dollar spent. It has been said that it is better to put a cheap plant into a well-dug hole than it is to put an expensive, high-quality plant in a poorly dug hole. In many situations that is true, but when it comes to analyzing the quality of a design's plant selections, the optimum result is found by placing the right plant, the right way, in just the right spot, to achieve the greatest desired effects. For a high caliber of plant section, we must assume that the plant selected is a high-quality plant and that it was planted correctly. The American Nurseryman's Association has developed national production standards to ensure that nurseries produce the highest-quality materials so that quality plants will be available to both designers and landscape contractors. These standards are found in the **American National Standards Institute (ANSI)** A60.1 standards for nursery stock.

NOTE: The quality of workmanship in landscape construction in the United States has produced large numbers of trees that are planted incorrectly, even by professional contractors. The improper planting of trees and shrubs will, over time, cause significant physical deterioration of trees and plants. While a detailed discussion of this issue is beyond the scope of this book, PAs should be aware of the problem and be able to make obsolescence deductions where it exists.

The goal of creating an appealing landscape space should incorporate many benefits. The selection of plants in the landscape design may improve real estate market value or salability, it may simply add beauty and enhance the use and enjoyment of a property to its owner, it may contribute to a healthy ecosystem and it may reduce the need for maintenance; there are vast tangible and intangible benefits that one can attain, just by selecting the right plants for the right spot.

Each plant will fulfill a specific functional and aesthetic need. The best designs will use plants that fulfill many functions and aesthetics synergistically. In aesthetics, we are concerned mostly with the visual roles that plants play, but the best designs are multisensory experiences that incorporate sounds, touch, fragrance and even taste. These sensory elements are intentionally woven to form an artistic framework where the art medium is made primarily of plants. The aim is to establish targeted and effective sensory diversity and depth in three dimensions. When immersed in a landscape where the plants are well selected, the landscape plantings will pique the user's interest and entice most of the user's senses. Plants can also unify landscaping by offering a transitional zone from one space to the next. Since various species of wildlife, like birds, butterflies, pollinators and others, are attracted to specific types of shelter and sources of food that specific plants provide, these can be selected to add other dynamics to a landscape that would otherwise be absent.

In addition to being a very large and beautiful display, southern magnolia emits a very desirable, powerful and perfume-like fragrance when in bloom.

Many native plants can provide regional and even historic elements to a design and high quality native plants can usually be obtained from growers that specialize in them. Likewise, there are many great non-native species that are well-adapted to North American sites. Those may offer unique qualities that are not found among the native plants. Great care should be taken to avoid aggressive and exotic species of plants that are capable of displacing other plants. This can create tremendous maintenance problems and if they escape the landscape into other environments, they can have devastating consequences, both ecologically and economically. The USDA has developed an exotic and invasive species list for each geographic location in the United States located at https://www.invasivespeciesinfo.gov/resources/databases.shtml.

Putting the right plant in the right space means the designer should understand the site conditions, the requirements of the plant and the desired design outputs. I've covered most of species adaptability characteristics in Chapter 3. It is vitally important for the PA to understand the abilities of plants to adapt, grow to maturity and to flower/fruit at the place and time selected. In design, adaptability is pivotal for allowing a plant's maximum delivery of designed benefits. Anything that diminishes this ability to deliver benefits is obsolescence. The plant appraiser should be able to objectively identify the benefits, be able to identify any deficiencies in the plant's ability to deliver benefits and calculate the deficiencies' importance in the appraisal process. The various methods of analyzing this information are covered in the Analysis section (Chapters 10–13) of this book.

Knowing how a plant or tree grows over time and anticipating how it will look in the beginning and how well it will fill the space provided over time is another critical consideration. We broadly describe this tendency to grow in certain fashion the growth-habit of a plant. It is important for plant appraisers to judge how well the intended design placement has anticipated the selected plants growth-habit, along with other intended deliverables. Plants should be the correct size, shape, form and texture at maturity as they fill the intended landscape space. The plant should provide interest without overpowering the space or burdening neighboring elements of the design. Sometimes functional benefits are intended to be more dominant, such as the transpirational cooling effect of a deciduous tree that overhangs a roof line, or the intent may be more aesthetic, such as an accent tree or foundation plant. Whatever the goal is, the measure of obsolescence is how well the tree delivers on it.

Mature size of trees and plants and their distance from structures are important design considerations. Spacing of plants near buildings should be one-half of their mature width plus one foot from the wall of a structure. Good design is planned with the desired mature size in mind versus poor design with a confined plant's need for constant pruning maintenance.

Another important consideration is seasonal interest. Professional design incorporates plants with seasonal cycles and colors that complement each other and provide year-round interest. Flowering trees provide pastels in spring and summer. Beds of perennials and annuals furnish vivid hues in spring, summer and fall and many deciduous plants offer bursts of color in fall. Some plants, like witch hazel and apricot, even bloom in winter, and many varieties of plants are selected for bark characteristics that are very showy when leaves are not present. Many plants have more attractive foliage than flowers. In addition to innumerable shades of green, leaves are bred and selected for a variety of other colors. Many plants have variegated leaves with multicolored or variegated leaf tissue. Some variegated leaves have stripes of different colors (usually white, cream, or yellow and green). Others have patches or blotches of color, including combinations of white, cream, or yellow and green; pink and purple; or yellow, orange, red and copper. All of this variation provides the architect with an almost infinite number of color combinations from which to choose.

Creating seasonal interest at the highest level requires careful consideration of each showy, aesthetic characteristic along with a plant's other characteristics. The important seasonal interest characteristics are: inflorescence color and timing; foliage texture, color and timing; fruiting color and timing; and bark texture color and timing. Selections over a variety of plants are made in strategic locations to achieve visual impacts in every season. For example, evergreen selections are made for base color near the foundation of buildings or as a backdrop to create contrast with seasonal show-offs.

This annual bed of tulips creates an impressive display of color in an otherwise uninteresting space.

Designs that provide year-round interest have the greatest aesthetic. A river birch *(Betula nigra)* has attractive spring flowers that develop before leaves, beautiful fall or midsummer color and attractive exfoliating (peeling and shedding) bark in winter. The effects can be powerful when planted en masse or planted as specimens while contrasted against an evergreen backdrop. Concentration of color is desired where accent plants are located in the design.

These catkins (flowers) offer a very early display that interesting enough to inspire curiosity.

While seasonal interest is critically important, when it comes to plant color, variety is not necessarily better. The main foundational colors, found in various shades of green, contrast and complement the seasonal accent colors. Too many evergreens in the design can be visually "heavy" and may not provide as much seasonal interest as can be developed in combination with deciduous plants.

This deciduous blackgum tree has an impressive display of blue fruit in fall/winter while the evergreens in the background serve as a backdrop to the blackgum's seasonal show.

This blue atlas cedar (Cedarus atlantica 'Glaca') offers blue-green colored foliage and interesting texture all winter long.

The design begins with identification of the site characteristics and establishment of the borders, screens and establishment of the locations where the landscape's important focal features will be. Once the overall placement of the main areas is laid out, specimen plantings are chosen as large and/or unusually impressive plants that are the planned focus of interest. Accent plants are located nearby to support the main specimen characteristics of interest and they help to define the space of the garden. Shrubs and trees with similar maintenance needs are typically grouped in beds of defined space and are planted in beds with curved edges. Poor design has a scattering of plants throughout a lawn or, even worse, divergent pairings of plants that are alternated in large plantings. Woody amenity landscape ornamentals and turfgrasses are segregated in professional design since trees and grass have very different needs. Finally, the use of large archways, pergolas and trellises consisting of perennial vines and ground plantings of cold hardy ornamentals and grasses can create organic winter forms and winter interest.

The final plant selections of well-developed architectural design are appropriate for the site and maximize the desired effects and impacts sought. For example, a tall, narrow growth-habit evergreen like emerald arborvitae *(Thuja occidentalis 'Emerald')* can, in time, establish a screen or a windbreak, but they can also serve as foundation plants to soften tall verti-

This privacy screen provides a visible barrier between the neighboring back yards.

cal edges of buildings that are situated in narrow spaces. Large deciduous trees planted in proximity to a building foundation on the south and west exposures can create significant shade to mitigate hot summer temperatures and may even provide relief from intense glare. Under the shade of such trees, masses of herbaceous shade-tolerant perennials like hosta lily *(Hosta sp.)*, foamflower *(Tiarella cordifolia)*, Lenten rose *(Hellaborus sp.)*, white wood aster *(Eurybia divaricatus)* and green-and-gold *(Chrysogonum virginianum)*, provide spectacular seasonal interest and are capable being grouped into a theme planting.

Since the plant selections of a design are abstractly conceived to fill a role in the architecturally designed concept, matching the environmental and aesthetic characteristics of the site to the adaptive and aesthetic characteristics of each plant is a matter of plant/site coordination and has direct impact on a plant's performance in effectively delivering of amenity benefits. Selecting the best genus and species for each specific locale in

The Lenten roses (Helleborus sp.) provide evergreen foliage with a persistent splash of pastel color. They are well adapted to shade conditions and are somewhat tolerant of variable soil moisture conditions.

the design requires careful and thoughtful consideration. There are several indispensable resources available to assist landscape architects in this effort. Also, each geographic region is unique and the plant appraiser is advised to seek out local authorities (colleagues, consultants, extension experts, growers and educators) and to seek out local references as valuable resources for identifying locally recommended plant selection options.

The architectural rendition accurately depicts mature plant sizes to scale to determine the quantities of plants that are needed to complete the landscape design. The design schematic is also a good means to identifying the theme of the design and is helpful in identifying the designer's original intent. Oftentimes, either the original design schematic is unavailable or there is significant deviation from the original due to scarcity of plant materials. In such cases, the plant appraiser must use their best-qualified judgments in evaluating the executed design selections in plant materials and their significance in the landscape.

Elements in Design

The aesthetic of landscape design involves much more than just good looks and a pleasing feel. It involves intentional strategy — the synergistic deployment of both the functional aspects of trees, plants and **hardscapes** combined with those characteristics that appeal to the eye, the nose, the sense of touch, the sounds and even those things that appeal to one's palate. There are some basic principles of landscape design that PAs may need to be familiar with and be competent to judge. Well-designed landscape elements enhance the value of trees and landscaping while design deficiencies depreciate value. The amount of appreciation or depreciation and the role of design in the overall function and aesthetics is a matter of judgment based on the skills, education, training and experience of the PA.

Scale

In any architectural design, this is a ratio or proportion between two or three dimensions like the height and spread of a tree compared to the three-dimensional size of a house. This also works in two dimensions when a view is framed by flanking tree trunks, the tree canopy overhead and the horizon below. The size and distance of an accent tree to a residential entryway would be another example of scale. A carefully planned landscape design will consider the mature height and spread of plants as they grow over time before including them in the design. In poorly scaled

This image demonstrates the effect of scale. The design places a group of progressively smaller accent plants in the foreground that obscures a large open area in the middle ground with a backdrop of much larger trees. The user feels a sense of transition without feeling suddenly exposed.

design, you can clearly see when full-grown shrubs and trees have become oversized for the space in which they were planted. When plants become too large for a space, the aesthetic of proportion and scale is diminished. The result is imbalanced bloating where one element can overwhelm the design. On the other hand, if plants are too small or if there are not enough of them to fill the space, they often look inappropriately out of balance or out of proportion.

Balance

Visually, a landscape design intentionally draws the eye toward or away from various viewpoints, creating the aesthetic effect of balance. When properly weighted, the various landscape design elements automatically draw the eye to focus on specimen plants or views of peak interest and beauty. If a design lacks balance or symmetry, the focal point will appear off-axis and out of balance. Balance can be achieved in many ways such as mirroring, like where a symmetrical entryway has the same planting on both sides. Balance can also be achieved by placing plants of various colors, textures and sizes to reach equilibrium on either side of a focal point. For example, an accent tree may have a small retaining wall on one side balanced by a small evergreen tree appropriately placed on the opposite side. Similarly, a large, soft-textured, light-colored tree may be balanced by several shrubs of heavier color and density. The possibilities of balance are as diverse as the people who enjoy creating landscape designs.

Good design offers a sense of balance. The Japanese maple tree on the left is balanced by the bench on the right with the brook as a fulcrum in the middle. Note the excellent use of accents all round.

Poor design feels out of balance. The overgrown shrubs, pear tree and driveway on the right overpower the rest of the site's architecture, creating a severe imbalance of design.

Grouping

Groupings are groups of plants that are arranged to form a single unit in effect. Street trees are a common form of grouping where the replication of the design pattern defines the space and creates focal points along perspective lines and create a variety of other aesthetic effects. This is also an important characteristic in landscapes where various elements of visual impact are drawn together to form one component that may be seen from many angles. Too much variety and alternating plants with variable characteristics causes incoherence of theme and contradicts the conceptual thrust of the grouping.

Perspective

From the time we first begin to perceive the world around us, our mind's eye develops a robust construct about the size, distance and color of the objects we see. Most of the subconscious perceptions we have about our spatial world are also reinforced continuously with our daily spatial experiences. It is possible to use visual cues to trick a landscape user's eye into seeing one thing where a difference exists in spatial reality. This is the power of perspective and when used effectively in landscape design, it can make a landscape appear larger than it is, or it can make an open space feel more intimate and enclosed. The use of distance can make coarse textured plants seem fine-textured and with softer, toned colors. The use of fine-textured plants in a transitional space can expand the perceived distance to plants and other objects behind them. Tapered objects and hardscaping can create the illusion of depth and distance. The use of bolder colors, textures and smaller

This grouping of trees creates a dramatic sunset silhouette contrasted against a featureless horizon and residential neighborhood homes.

The descending curve in this wall creates the illusion that the bench is much farther away than it is.

sizes close in, with more subdued and larger plants farther away, can make a space feel and look much larger than it is. The opposite technique can be used to make a space feel smaller and more intimate.

Repetition of Design

The patterns of a design are crucial to the development of a theme and the overall enjoyment of the intended aesthetic. The more a landscape element is repeated, the more powerful the effect becomes. While repetition is crucial, too much repetition is tedious. There must be a balance between the creative development of the space and pattern developed within that space.

In this public park, four baseball fields have walkways and greenspace between. Lacebark elms trees were planted on both sides of each walkway and this was repeated many times — 86 trees in all.

Accent

Professional landscape architectural design includes focal areas of interest and larger areas of static or dull-green canvas. These dull areas may be enhanced with plants that stand out against the backdrop. Accent trees and shrubs create orderly, non-focal interest where a void of creativity should not exist. Accent trees may also be used to accentuate the desirable character of specimen trees or they may be used to create curved lines instead of straight lines. A common example is the marriage of unnatural, long, straight, vertical, or horizontal lines of a structure to the natural, curved and rounded lines of foundation plants. Foundation plants soften the artifactual edges of structures and create a sense of belonging with nature. The effect is the building appears as coexisting in harmony with nature. Failure to use accent trees where they are needed results in poorer quality design as does the overuse of accents. The best design uses just the right number of accents to achieve the desired effect.

Designed Placement in Four Dimensions

Trees and landscaping deliver their benefits through four dimensions and the senses. Three dimensions are used to organize site space and the landscape architect's goal is to plan geometry so that functional and aesthetic delivery of benefits is maximized over the fourth dimension of time. The overhead character and form of trees defines the ceiling of an outdoor space. The canopy protects from the elements and provides a sense of security. The area directly under the canopy of a tree creates an enclosure of sorts. As the sun traverses the sky, the reflected sunlight can create a visual experience in color and character where the sun's movement is directed by tree as it casts shade on under-

Residential landscape design is developed in two dimensions, but in execution, landscape design is constructed in three dimensions plus the dynamic dimension of time.

story plants and structures. Trees also create a transition as one moves from under the canopy to an uncovered space and back under the protection of the tree canopy. This affect not only happens to people but also livestock and wildlife. These effects change dynamically throughout the daylight hours. They may also be enjoyed at night with the addition of moonlight or artificial lighting. These characteristics also change over time with the seasons of the year.

Focal Points

Carefully selected and placed plants or objects can direct a person's attention to a particular line of sight. This type of landscape planning stimulates movement and invites people moving through the space to decide the direction they will go beyond the point of their current perspective. Focal points are used in conjunction with screens and other background features to diminish the visual impact of areas beyond and around the focal point to draw greater attention. Focal points often signal that a change in scenery or experience will be offered to those who choose to head in that direction. A focal point should tease the user's senses by offering a unique and interesting feature that truly stands out. A well-placed focal point reveal leads the user on a pleasantly unexpected journey. The focal point is inviting. It is not a contrived manipulation to coerce the user. The garden story unfolds as one enters and this story continues to unfold as the guideway directs the user through the various landscape elements. The focal points suggest what might be a new experience so that users feel a sense of anticipation as they approach decision points along the path. The focal point also hints at a destination — the garden activity where climax of theme is revealed in full glory. From the theme climax reveal, there is a transition to the next destination. Specimen trees or plants often serve as focal points.

Pattern Language

Developed by Christopher Alexander, pattern language articulates recognizable patterns in nature and human society that have emerged in the collaboration of nature and mankind over the ages. The underpinning philosophy of pattern language is that patterns affect and influence how people live — they either consciously or unconsciously affect what we think, the decisions we make and the way we behave. Dr. Alexander studied patterns in nature and developed social pattern concepts from those natural observations. He sought to influence societal lifestyles,

The striking pattern of this stone wall was balanced by the surrounding landscaping, which was natural, fluid and had no repeating patterns at all.

communities and architecture. Patterns come in an endless variety and we experience them many times each day. Patterns enhance the garden experience of the user

The human eye is very limited. While we can perceive motion at wide angles of about 170 degrees, only a small portion of that field of view can be seen in focused detail at any given time. We can only take in and process a small fraction of all the light information that is visible from the world around us. Maslow's hierarchy of needs underscores our natural tendency to see what is closest to us first, so we tend to look in the foreground with greater attention to detail and focus. Things further away in the background have a lower need priority and tend to remain out of our focal detail range. We see the background pattern is there, but it is usually not seen in great detail. The study of patterns and their potential applications in landscaping are important to function and use of spaces by people. PAs do well to recognize design patterns for their contribution to the landscape space.

The white, green and red pattern seen here in this planting of dwarf Burford hollies is a common pattern in nature that signifies shelter and food in mid-winter for many wildlife creatures.

Garden Geometry

Geometry is another feature of our world that can have great influence on where and how we live. The ancient Egyptians built the pyramids and many great architectural edifices to their gods. Their entire society was built around these great geometric structures. The geometry of Egyptian pyramids and other large objects intersects with the vast desert plane, creating a relationship that reflects on earth what can be seen in the heavens on a grand scale. Likewise, there is a relationship between the shape of objects like the Sphinx (which was created by man) and natural contour of the earth surrounding it. In the case of the pyramids, man creates the supernatural effect of contrast between the earth and the pyramids, just as there is a natural contrast between the earth and the heavens. The placement of the Pyramids of Giza creates a supernatural contrast and a connection to the stars in the constellation of Orion's belt. Also, the placement of the pyramids next to the Nile River mirrors the same spacing of Orion's belt to the Milky Way in the night sky.

In this architectural theme, the design incorporates images of human beings existing in harmony with nature as the inanimate metal sculpture encompasses the live tree trunk. In turn, the human imitates the architects theme.

Oftentimes, the geometry of the garden and the geometry of the architectural structures in and around the garden create contrasts or a marriage of nature and the man-made elements. Depending on the architectural theme, the landscaping effort should emphasize that contrast of nature to man or, more commonly, the landscaping effort should create harmony between the two.

Geometry of objects in the space must relate to the limitations imposed by the location of boundaries and the desired/required activities within the space. The PA should ask, is the geometry appropriate for the anticipated activity in that space? As the invisible perspective lines extend out from a building at various angles, the design should anticipate where the eye will naturally migrate to where the perspective lines converge. Perspective lines will converge where the corner of the building meets the ground or sky, or where the center line of the window or door meets an open lawn space, or where the edge of a porch is in relation to a background screening hedge of vegetation. The landscape should have an appropriate connection with the structure. Most often, the landscape design effort is made to soften the architectural outline of a building with the soft-textured, natural foliage of evergreen plants. Placement of a distinctive flowering specimen tree at a distant convergence from the centerline of a large window creates a focal point when seen from within the building or outside of a building when standing near the window.

The soft texture, adaptability and slow growth of this evergreen boxwood shrub make it an ideal foundation plant. Because of its slow growth and tolerance to pruning, it also makes an excellent hedge.

Created spaces in landscape design come in great variety of themes. Each landscape has unique characteristics that can add or take away value to the user's landscape experience. Carefully planned landscapes that employ appropriate geometry enjoy added value. When geometry is poorly designed to the space, less value is delivered.

Fundamental Principles of Good Design

Like art, landscape design is comprised of various elements that are brought together in a theme that is aesthetically appealing. The composition of the design follows fundamental principles that allow each element to smoothly contribute appropriately to the overall theme. This is true for each composite section of the landscape, as well as the entire landscape design. Simplicity, variety and replication, all work to harmonize an overall effect that the architect wants to communicate.

This landscape was simplified by removing a large and very messy birch tree that was poorly placed over the main entry walkway. (See stump next to the stone walk).

Simplicity

Less is more when it comes to landscape design. Simplicity is easy on the eye. It also limits the size of plantings, the number or variety of plants that are used to create a space. Simplicity leaves room for the user's imagination to fill a space and it averts that over-filled sensation of having too much going on. Simplicity incorporates groupings of plants en masse, constrained by simple lines and curves to garner greater impact and interest. Simplicity avoids the distracting overuse of many patterns or irregular or shape-angled lines.

Replication

There is a fine line between replication and monotony. Replication simplifies but does so only to the extent that it affects unity of the theme. Over-replication can become monotone and humdrum. Good design is always interesting and unified. Poor design is either too busy, discontinuous or dull.

Line Forms

Our eyes are naturally drawn to points were lines or implied lines converge. Line forms define spaces and draw the user's eye by grouping plants or other elements. The unconscious force of line form directs our attention through the various geometric flows of the design space and draw contrast between the upright and level fields of view.

Variety

Where simplicity creates unity, variety creates interest. Both unity and variety are exemplified in the Chinese principles of Feng Shui, the Eastern system of rules that govern spatial arrangement and orientation in relation to the flow of metaphysical (spiritual) energy through space. The favorable effects of this unseen but felt flow of metaphysical energy is manifest when design strikes the balance between unity and variety. Too much emphasis on either unity or variety can also be felt as an undesirable effect.

Too much variety creates disunity and disharmony. The unique character of each species and cultivar in this site is lost in the business of the design. There must be balance between variety and simplicity.

The variety of this landscape creates interest but is in danger of being out of balance and in disharmony with the remainder of the landscape. The central focus of the specimen tree dominates all else, creating a need for some varietal interest.

The essence of Feng Shui is exemplified in variety, harmony and balance. In this subject, we have the elevated terrestrial spacing and weight of plant material in harmony with the rock garden below that simulates the nature of water. Both elements are weighted so that there is a sense of flow from the upper elevation to the lower elevation (from left to right in the back-middle ground of the image and curving around from right to left in the foreground). With each part of the landscape contributing to the whole, the harmonic balance between variety and unity is displayed.

Harmony

Feng Shui guidance also serves to balance all the design principles. This is achieved when individual design components are brought together as an interconnected, harmonious whole. Each part connects to and complements the others as the user moves from space to space. The user feels a sense of harmony among the component parts.

Designed Minimization of Maintenance

An important goal in landscape architectural design is efficient and less frequent maintenance that reduces the costs associated with landscape care. Landscape architects avoid sharp angles, corners and narrow patches of lawn that require the lawn equipment operator to make several angled movements when cutting grass. Irregular edges around the base of trees are replaced with sweeping bed edges that are easy to mow and water.

Candytuft makes an excellent bed edge material. It is slow growing, highly adaptable to a wide range of growing conditions and has an impressive and persistent white inflorescence display in spring.

Lawns are among the most labor, machine and material intensive landscape features. Lawns require regular mowing and watering — sometimes several per week. They also require other maintenance tasks and more fertilizer than higher plants and they require far more chemical and pesticide inputs. Increasing the number of trees and shrubs reduces the size of lawn areas and dramatically reduces the costs of maintenance.

Plants with the right growth habit characteristics and the right mature size will minimize pruning and shearing to maintain the desired size and shape and reduce maintenance costs. Likewise, deploying **drought**-tolerant plants, wind-resistant selections, or plants adapted to low fertilization and insect/disease resistance saves on maintenance costs. It is easier and less costly to maintain plants when they are grown together with other

Lawns require far more intensive maintenance than do other types of landscaping. This lawn has smooth curves and no sharp corners that would require the operator to stop and maneuver during mowing operations. Note the line geometry and how it affects the overall theme of the design.

plants that have similar cultural needs (like pruning, watering and fertilizing). By keeping landscape materials such as mulches and composts near to where they are used most and keeping recycled organic waste near to where maintenance equipment is stored, the cost of hauling materials and other maintenance tasks are made more efficient.

Minimizing the removal of grass clippings and other organic material from the landscape site is a great time and money-saving approach. Since many trimmings and other waste can be converted into nutrient-rich mulches, these efforts should be performed as close as possible to where they will be used to provide the most benefit. Some examples include the use of mulching mower blades to cut grass, allowing fallen leaves to serve as biodegradable bed mulch and using wood chips for pathways and playgrounds.

Designing for Wildlife Conservation

The structure and composition of woodlands and forests will change over time in a process called succession. A clear-cut site will eventually become an old-growth forest given enough time. Certain wildlife will be favored at a site as different successional stages of trees create new habitats corresponding to the same successional stages of animals. For exam-

Dogwoods, as understory trees, are one of the most desirable ornamentals because of their beautiful flower displays in spring, their impressive red leaf display in the fall and their beautiful red fruit display in winter. The fruit is also an important food source for small animals and birds.

Hollow stumps like the one pictured here are vital habitat for small to medium-sized wildlife species.

ple, early-successional woodlands have more fruit, seeds and edible woody material for birds and small animals but will have fewer nuts, acorns and cavity trees than late-successional forests where larger animals live. Depending on the type of management that is applied to the land, successional stages can be either maintained or created to provide habitat for different groups of wildlife. (Morrison M., 2006)

Succession in landscaping also has a dramatic effect on the amount and variety of wildlife that will inhabit a site. Through careful planning, layers of habitat can be developed to attract wildlife across the ecological spectrum. Songbirds and small mammals thrive in habitat that contains wildflowers, grasses and berry-producing plants. Hard mast-producing trees provide habitat for turkey, deer and larger birds of prey. As the landscape grows taller with denser canopy cover, it will naturally provide habitat for larger and higher successional creatures. Even things like water features, hollow trees, tree stumps and logs provide important habitats for large numbers of wildlife.

To enhance the vertical structure of woodlands, it is important to keep understory and mid-story vegetation intact. Forest animals usually specialize on layers of the forest, depending on these components for foraging or nesting substrates. Although removing shrubs and saplings creates an open, park-like structure, it will prohibit some understory-dependent plant and animal species from using the area. Overstory trees are used by a variety of birds for foraging and nesting. (Morrison M., 2006)

Ecologically Based Design Considerations

Landscape designs are part of a much larger community of plants with wide and varied use and applications. Environmentally friendly landscapes protect a site's natural elements and develop the landscape as a living ecosystem with various successional levels of habitat. Aims of these efforts include reducing energy, water and materials inputs and avoiding the use of pesticides and prohibited materials. Environmentally friendly design techniques and considerations describe ecosystem service characteristics in the landscape.

Succession

It may seem intuitive, but plants get bigger over time. As they do so, plants and trees will occupy space to the exclusion of other plants, trees and even structures. When unmanaged, this phenomenon causes a cascade of physical changes to the environment that are collectively called succession. Succession is long-term and causes ecological communities to undergo changes, in more or less orderly and predictable ways. Successional changes following a large-scale site disturbance begin with pioneering plants and concludes with apex forest habitat. Typically, this process begins with new plantings or the initial colonization of a new land form with highly adaptable plant species.

Professional landscape architectural design is based on the mature size of the plants. Young plants are given plenty of space to grow to their full sizes and may take many years to mature. Effective design and planning takes the successional stages of selected plants into account. In execution, a landscape architectural design is more than simply planting. It is planting followed by years and years of maintenance. Early designs often have more plants then are necessary for the highest levels of succession where some thinning is both planned and appropriate. Some designs call for mulched beds around newly planted evergreens, but as some evergreens mature, they occupy space all the way to the ground. Soon they fill the entire bed and eliminate the need for maintenance mulching.

A good example is white pine *(Pinus strobus)*. As a young tree, white pine can form an excellent privacy hedge or screen. As it matures for the first fifteen years or so, this tree grows tall and wide to the ground. After this early growth period, it reaches it maximum canopy width of about 30 feet and begins to encounter **inner canopy dieback** where the lower branches (lacking in sustainable sunlight) die and eventually fall off. This changes the character of the tree into a more upright and stately form, eventually exposing the attractive trunk bark and transforming the tree into a border or perhaps a **mutual property boundary** tree or some other purpose that defines the space with a dramatically different aesthetic.

When plants become overcrowded, they are more susceptible to stress, predation by insects and diseases. Stress causes plants to become very unattractive, maintenance-intense and may eventually necessitate removals to improve plant health. In successional development of a site, changes in successional plant species are brought about by ever increasing competition for light, water and other resources. Taller growth-habit species typically have the advantage, so successional advancement usually coincides with dominance of the vertical space.

This sample of dried wood has deep grooves (called galleries) where destructive wood boring insects burrowed under the bark and encircled the trunk. They may have caused the demise of this tree.

Designing with Synergy

Some edibles have very desirable aesthetic qualities. Blueberries *(Vaccinum sp.)*, for example, have spring flowers offer light-green foliage, dark-blue blueberries and intense-orange, fall leaf display. Cranberries *(Viburnum sp.)* have impressive spring flowers and excellent fall color. Many species also have unusual or interesting foliage textures. The use of herbs as **ground cover**s or bed edges is well established. The variety of edibles that can be incorporated into the landscape is astonishing.

The use of edibles makes efficient use of space through synergistic broadening of aesthetics to the garden. The same concept can provide food as habitat, provide a source for cut flowers and may attract a variety of pollinators. It is not necessary to substitute edible plants for all ornamentals, but many edible woody landscape plants have high ornamental potential. The goal is to expand the garden to develop sensory perception beyond the visual aesthetic. By selecting a variety of plants that ripen at different times throughout the year, seasonal interest is peaked.

Many edible plants have impressive flowers, foliage, fruit, or fall color like this blueberry (Vaccinium sp.), which has all four aesthetic attributes.

CHAPTER EIGHT

Identification of Landscape Use Benefits Characteristics

The aesthetic use benefits are qualitative landscape user deliverables that will be analyzed for efficiency (obsolescence) by the appraiser. They are limited by various things, such as poor landscape architectural design placement and poor plant species/site selection.

In practice, the PA must be credible and relevant by performing the following for each use:

Describe the plant's aesthetic characteristics and benefits in sufficient detail that they may be reasonably perceived in use to provide value to an owner or interested party.

Evaluate the effectiveness of the plant's role in providing the aesthetic benefits described; identify any deficiencies in that aesthetic benefit role.

Apply any warranted obsolescence in a weighted deduction for the deficiency in the plant appraisal process.

Shade Trees

Shade trees are cultivated for the specific use of shade. This term usually applies to large deciduous trees with spreading canopies. Some of the most popular shade trees are oaks, maples, sycamore, birches and elms, but there are many others.

Specimen Plants

Specimen plants should be selected for their size or qualitative characteristics, not quantity. Since specimen plants are usually grown singly for ornamental effect, rather than being massed with other plants, they are intended to create narrower focal points and draw attention to a specific area. Trees and plants do this effectively when they have interesting and unusual attributes — specimens are often striking in their appearance.

Above: The specimen trees of this front yard create a park-like experience.

Right: The specimen tree in this photo is the main feature and would be the main feature of any landscape. This particular tree is a champion and is the largest tree for many miles around. It is situated in a residential neighborhood that is bordered by industrial complexes, municipal buildings and public housing.

Seasonal Color/Foliage Persistence

Shade trees that are selected for their seasonal color interest or foliage persistence should be evaluated on how well their characteristics accomplish their intended use in the landscape. Effective shade tree color/persistence will present the user with dramatic effect. With color, this will occur while the tree is in bloom or when leaves change in the fall. An evergreen's effectiveness is measured by how well the foliage presents to the user consistently throughout the year.

Evergreen trees can offer persistent foliage color throughout the year, creating a more static contrast to other dynamic elements of the landscape.

Screening

Ornamental **landscape screens** are comprised of plants or trees that are strategically placed to define a space or partition an area within the landscape. Often, they provide a backdrop and/or block a view to draw the eye's attention to a focal point in the landscape. There are three ways that a landscape screen can effectively mitigate an undesirable view: privacy, diminishment and perspective.

First, the screen can obscure the undesirable view by placing large, dense vegetation directly between the undesirable view and the eye, thus creating a backdrop onto which the architect may place more interesting plants. Second, the screen can diminish the impact of an undesirable view by placing large vegetation that is aesthetically pleasing and that consists of interesting colors, textures and shapes that draw the eye away from an undesirable vista; thus, the eye is naturally and subconsciously drawn to something desirable instead of something undesirable in the background. Thirdly, the screen can be used to change the focal point of the eye through perspective. By placing attractive plants at strategic points at a distance along perspective lines the focal point of the eye unconsciously changes focus to the more attractive plants. This adds a perception of depth to the scenery and causes the eyes' focus to diminish the impact of the out-of-focus background. This is because the eye is automatically drawn to objects that follow natural lines of perspective. The effect is that proper placement of plants will generate a focal point of reference away from other points, causing undesirable objects that are farther away to be obscured or out of focus. A screen may be effective by merely diminishing the impact of undesirable objects or views.

This is especially true where appropriate trees and shrubs are placed between the user and power lines or other undesirable views located at a distance. The view of power lines is easily obscured or diminished with

Landscape screens diminish the visual impact of undesirable background views by drawing the eye to more pleasing and interesting foreground imagery. In this image, the retaining wall, fences, structures and utility boxes are diminished while the plants and tree trunk draw attention close in.

careful placement and plant selection in the landscape design. It is also important to recognize that trees growing near power lines often grow within vegetation management right-of-way easements and that trees requiring vegetation management activity may have less value because of restrictions/limitations imposed on their size.

Buffer

According to the National Arbor Day Foundation, trees can have a dampening effect on noise pollution. A tree buffer can significantly reduce road noise. Several factors can influence the effectiveness trees as a means of noise attenuation. The first factor that contributes to the effectiveness of a tree buffer to attenuate noise is the density of tree's foliage. The second is the persistence of their foliage and the third is the size of the noise buffer. A 150-foot buffer of evergreen trees is needed to reduce car noise from 80 dBs to 65 dBs

While not as well researched, the frequency of noise plays an important role in the need for mitigation. It is possible to alter the frequency of noise, without a significant reduction in noise volume, to effectively

These 110 deodar cedars were planted in a green space between a residential neighborhood and a nearby skate park. While the overall noise reduction from the park was nominal, the frequency of the noise was significantly reduced.

mitigate it. This is because the human ear is particularly sensitive to certain noise frequency ranges. Evenly planting, a small tree buffer can alter and diffuse noise frequencies from higher sensitivity range to lower sensitivity frequency ranges. This is affected by the shape, density, size and spacing of the planting and by the species habit and leaf characteristics.

While noise attenuation may be considered a functional benefit, as a buffer aesthetic, trees can present a significant feeling of security and privacy when the owner knows that there is an area of vegetation between his/her property and a noise-generating site, like a highway. Even if the decibel noise reduction of a buffer cannot be easily measured for effectiveness, the presence of a buffer may still be effective as it is perceived by its owner.

Frame Vista Vertical/Horizontal

In sites where a distant view is desirable, the professional landscaping effort is always made to accentuate and enhance the desirable view. This effort is referred to as framing. Typically, evergreen plants are selected and placed along the extended horizon in progressively smaller increments starting with the largest plants on the outer extent and smallest at the

These ancient cedar trees frame the view from the patio that exist behind the beautiful wrought iron railing and they frame the view from the balcony beyond it. The foresight and planning that went into this design was advanced.

Another view from farther back shows the extent of framing repetitions.

opposite edge. The effect is that the user's eye is automatically drawn to put the desirable view in focus. This can be a powerful use of shade trees.

Vista pruning of trees and shrubs may be required to maintain the view and framing effects. In some areas of the country and in a variety of homeowner's associations, the view is protected by ordinance or covenant and the vegetation that obscures a view in such situations may be less valuable because of the restrictions on plant size.

Define Public Space

Trees are often used to define public spaces. Street trees provide a special aesthetic that may be enjoyed by all users, public and private. Street trees are found along sidewalks, in the medians of boulevards and along streets everywhere. The benefits of such plantings are both functional and aesthetic and there are many of them. The benefits these trees provide in use must be weighed against the safety of motorists with their proximity to high-speed travel. Street trees have higher maintenance costs where canopy height and distance from roadways and sidewalks must be maintained and where visual site distances are required for roadway traveler safety. Canopy cover can also limit the size of vehicles that can pass along a street, requiring special signage and travel restrictions of oversized trucks. While the benefits of trees provide value, limitations can pose a liability or a design deficiency can limit benefits delivery.

The mature trees of this site define the space.

Trees in parks are used to define space in a variety of ways. Many of these uses correspond to the uses provided in landscape architecture, but parks are often designed with athletic fields and open, grassy spaces so that large numbers of people can gather with unobstructed views. These open spaces are typically lined with large trees that indicate to users where the gathering points or open use spaces are located. The large variety of benefits that are provided by park trees must be weighed against their proximity to people and the frequency of which the trees are near people. An appropriate amount of maintenance is required to keep park trees safe. High numbers of defects and high **failure rated**-conditioned trees or very poor condition-rated trees can pose a special liability or a deficiency in design.

Accent Trees

Accent trees fill the in-between space and help to develop areas of focus. In other forms of art, we refer to these accents as highlights and shadow. The composite elements in the landscape design should create harmony and accent trees and shrubs are most useful in that effort. Accent plants may be used to draw attention to a landscape feature, such as an opening to a walkway, seating, landscape surround experience, statuary or other plants. Specimens are individual accents that display some showy characteristic.

Garden statuary does not need to be particularly large to be effective. These tulips and pansies provide an excellent accent to the whimsical subject of the monument.

Accents are used singly or in groups to add emphasis to a feature or are used along perspective lines to draw the eye through the landscape. Depending on their function and use, accents are placed in fashion that maximizes the intended effect. A variety of plant characteristics can be used to achieve this effect, such as color, texture, plant size, habit, leaf persistence and bark character.

The stately character of the oak tree trunk is accented by the beautiful fall display of the understory dogwood nearby. Both plants border the walkway and create a pleasing aesthetic to the user.

The boundary hedge of Japanese variegated privet creates an impressive barrier that also accents the magnolia tree near the structure. The inflorescence is both showy and very fragrant. While this impressive plant seems well suited for its purpose, Privet species are considered an exotic invasive pest in some areas and since they are in the olive family, the abundant fruit is a poor food source for wildlife.

Barrier

Accent trees and shrubs serve several aesthetic barrier applications in landscape design. When it comes to living barriers, privacy hedges are typical and they are normally used to control the flow of pedestrian traffic. There are other forms of structural barriers such as walls, fences, gates and doors that need to be integrated into the surrounding landforms through the addition of tree and shrub plantings or through structural abutment to buildings or both. Barriers are placed to limit movement between desperate elements of the landscape design and to maintain the flow of movement for the desired aesthetic effect in landscape use. Like screens, they also serve as a screen to hide undesirable views or to hide the storage of landscape maintenance machinery, tools or materials.

Create Contrast Interest

When specimens are unusually large or have other unique characteristics, accent trees and shrubs can provide contrast to the specimen that helps users to focus on the specimen's characteristics or they accentuate the distinguished characteristic to make it appear more impressive. Landscape accents may be the landscape point of interest, especially when there is a large backdrop of larger evergreens or if there is a large, featureless wall in the background.

Draw Attention

Sometimes there are elements in a landscape that could easily be missed if not for the addition of an accent plant. Accents draw attention through various means and aid the user by revealing landscape elements that might otherwise go unnoticed.

The fine texture and color of these cut-leaf Japanese maple leaves draw attention while simultaneously achieving softness in the design.

Transitional Layering

With any landscape design, there must be space between elements of interest. These spaces may be layered to create a smooth transition and take the users from one space to the next with some measure of patterned emphasis and repetition. Accent use at different depths and heights go a long way toward developing transitional space effectively.

Add Depth

Any open space that is not intended to produce a focal effect is a candidate for accent plantings. A common use of accents in an open area is to create the illusion of depth. To create more depth to a space, the design incorporates progressively larger or progressively smaller species with similar characteristics along natural perspective lines.

Define Space

While shade trees are often used to define space in parks and along streets and other large areas, accent trees may be used to perform a similar function in the landscape where space is more limited. See Define Public Space.

Seasonal Color–Foliage Persistence

See Landscape Uses of Shade Trees.

Shrubs

Uses of landscape shrubs are as limitless as the imaginations of the professionals engaged in landscape design efforts. By far, the most common use of evergreen shrubs is as foundation plantings for structures. Other shrubs are used as accents, specimens or hedges and they are frequently used to create garden patterns.

Ground Covers and Vines

Ground covers and vines are used as their names imply. Found along the edges of beds and pathways, these plants offer transitional layering at the lowest level of vertical space. They form flower gardens and habitats in a variety of settings. It is important to distinguish landscape ornamentals that have desirable qualities and weeds that have very undesirable qualities.

From the lowest levels to the vertical and overhead space vines offer creative versatility.

Ancillary Features

Landscaping beyond the plant life also has functional and aesthetic value. These features include walls, patios, decks, pergolas, steps, pathways driveways, water features, lighting and irrigation systems. If the plant appraisal problem calls for opinions about the ancillary features of landscapes, the plant appraiser should be able to identify the relevant characteristics of the ancillary feature, identify the functional and aesthetic benefits that these characteristics provide, identify any deficiencies that exist in the ancillary features and apply those deficiencies in benefit delivery as obsolescence.

See "Field Data of Amenity Plant Appraisal Characteristics" worksheet, Appendix A-1.

Water features can be an important element in landscape design. The sounds and movement can create a profoundly stimulating aesthetic.

CHAPTER NINE

Identification of Limitations to Plant Value

Litter

While a tree may not meet the legal standard of a nuisance merely because it encroaches onto another's property, casts a shadow onto a neighbor, obstructs a neighbor's view, or drops fruit, leaves, twigs and other **litter** onto a neighbor, some trees are messier than others and they consume more maintenance resources to clean-up after them. Depending on the situation (like a large weeping willow *(Salix babylonica)* or river birch *(Betula nigra)* planted next to a patio or deck), trees that produce litter daily and sometimes hourly, require constant clean-up. In sites with high rates of occupancy, litter may be a source of obsolescence. The extra maintenance required to keep an area free of litter may reach the level of a design deficiency where some form of obsolescence is warranted. Plant appraisers should be aware of this potential and be able to account for it in the professional plant appraisal process when obsolescences exist.

Excessive Growth

Some plants grow faster than others. When plants grow too large for the planned design space, pruning is needed to reduce plant size. Pruning is also needed to improve the health and structure of many plants. Some common examples are plants in the Rose *(Rosaceae)* family (which includes all fruit trees and, of course, roses) and many species of euonymus (*Euonymus sp.*) require frequent pruning. While many of these plants have very attractive characteristics, the speed at which they grow can create a need for extra maintenance to keep them healthy and appealing. When the placement of such plants is such that the plant quickly outgrows the design space without continual pruning, it may reach the level of a designed deficiency. This problem may also arise in landscapes that have large numbers of fast-growing plants that tend to grow with poor structure. Plant appraisers should be aware of this potential problem and be able to account for it in the professional plant appraisal process.

Hazard Trees and Risk

When identifying and judging the condition characteristics in plant appraisal, GPA9 suggests that trees with a **condition rating** of 50% or less may be hazardous and should be evaluated for potential risks. Identifying and managing the risks associated with trees in urban areas is a subjective process that is fraught with uncertainty and, therefore, requires extensive local experience and a high level of professional judgment. Since the nature of tree failures remains largely unknown, our ability to predict which trees will fall and in which fashion is very limited.

As practiced in the past, tree hazard evaluation and **risk assessment** involves the following considerations:

- The potential of the tree to fall
- The environment that may contribute to failure
- The potential **target(s)**
- The likelihood and consequences of a tree failure's impact on the target

The essence of contemporary tree hazard evaluation is found in examining a tree for **structural defects.** Those defects that are associated with known patterns of failure are analyzed and the degree of risk is calculated based

This severe defect of the trunk, its proximity to the structure, the likelihood of failure impact and the severity of the potential loss made this tree very hazardous. The interior of the tree was completely hollow, and the tree did not show any visible signs that it was hazardous before a crack appeared after a storm.

on various factors such as the environment, the targets and the amount and likelihood that impact damage, injury or death will occur. For these reasons, hazard tree evaluation is not limited to tree **failure potential** alone.

AUTHOR'S NOTE: Currently, the ISA endorses Tree Risk Assessment Qualification (TRAQ) and ANSI A300 (Part 9) Tree Risk Assessment as the most recent advancements for the tree care industry. These resources are touted as a consensus standard of practice for assessing tree structure. While there are many advantages to using such methodology, discussing them is beyond the scope of this book. The author is intimately familiar with previously accepted tree hazard evaluation techniques and finds them minimally suitable for PAL purposes.

In ISO standards, the basis of risk management is predicated on risk assessment, or more simply put, the analysis of probabilities of various types and classifications of risks are typically segregated into clearly defined and measurable risks categories. ISO requires that known data/facts are analyzed and calculated using standard methodology and standardized analytics are used to broadly categorize threats for their use in risk management. These core ISO standard methods and analysis are not widely known to arborists and tree care professionals. The author does not endorse consensus standards that do not conform to well-established ISO risk analysis standards.

Hazard tree evaluation and risk analysis cannot be made solely based on scientific observations and calculations themselves; there is simply too much uncertainty. Currently, there is no rudimentary formula that can calculate tree risks to scientifically accepted standard deviations, nor is there ever likely to be. Regardless of this limitation that uncertainty places on tree risk assessment tasks, these tasks must be performed. **Consulting arborist**s services are critically important to assist tree owners in their decision making. Tree hazard evaluations and analyses must be done. They must also be conducted in the light of broad, local experience and a deep knowledge and understanding of tree failure patterns and indicators.

People need to know if the decisions they make about their trees are reasonable, if their trees are safe enough or not and what the potential consequences of a course of action might be. Issues of critical importance are the foreseeable consequences of a tree failure that could lead to property damage losses or a personal injury or a death.

Tree risk assessment professionals inform decision makers as to what is or is not reasonable action regarding tree hazards as they pertain to protecting people and property from falling trees or tree parts. Since the presence of tree hazards may affect value, PAs may be called upon to help decide if the costs of mitigation and/or the value of remainder trees are worth the safety mitigation efforts that would be performed.

Over 30 hazard/risk assessment methods have been developed and applied to the assessment of hazard trees. The commonly accepted method used by arborists in the evaluation of hazard trees is the one currently published by the ISA and has become one of the requirements of arborist certification. (ISA, 2008)(Gliman, 2004) In 2011, **TCIA** authored the "ANSI **A300** Part 9 Tree Risk Assessment a. Tree Structure Assessment" standard. That same year, the ISA developed an A300 Part 9 companion publication "Tree Risk Assessment **Best Management Practices**," a practical guide to performing tree risk assessment. While the hazard tree evaluation and risk assessment of tree appraisal assignments may conform to the ANSI A300 Part 9 standard, this standard by itself does not conform to **International Standards Organization (ISO)** 30000 for **Risk Management** or ISO 31000 for Risk Analysis. (Tree Care Industry Association, Inc., 2011).

In the ISA method, it is assumed that almost all trees pose some risk of failure. As the tree grows larger and more mature, the degree of risk increases. The challenge for arborists is to inform tree managers what is at risk and what level of risk is reasonable. The risk threshold that any owner/manager is willing to live with can only be determined by the property owner or manager, absent any intervention by the courts or a governmental authority. When weighing the potential risks against the potential benefits a subject tree will deliver over time, a tree owner/manager will often call in experts to help them understand fully the potential benefits and consequences of any decision to either retain or remove large trees. Consulting arborists must frequently make recommendations about the level of risk that a potential tree hazard poses to people or property weighted against the amenity value of a tree, and make recommendations that are reasonable in relation to the risk threshold. When the ability to mitigate the risk is so diminished that the risk remains too high to meet the test for reasonableness, the arborist must recommend tree removal.

The uncertainty of tree risk assessment is always high, partly because defects are not always visible through visual examination. Defects that are hidden inside the tree, behind foliage, or hidden by some other below ground obstruction cannot be considered for risk without careful inspection, testing or analysis. Additionally, natural forces are unpredictable and all factors that contribute to a failure are not known and/or cannot be known until after a failure has occurred. With experience and training, consulting arborist can learn to recognize patterns of failure that will help them recognize risks and aid in development of strategies to minimize or avoid tree risks.

Also, many types of tree failures are not well studied or understood and there are huge gaps in our understanding of the dynamic forces that we know exist but do not fully understand how they cause failures. Be it combined wind, weather and tree defects, or other unknowns, we only know, with certainty, the results when trees fail.

Inspection for tree hazards involves a great deal more than a casual stroll among them. Tree inspection is a systematic process of visually identifying risk factors and failure patterns and, when warranted, performing more detailed testing and analysis. It is not necessary or even possible to perform exhaustive testing on every tree. In fact, the need for additional testing beyond the visual inspection is rare. If there is a serious defect that fits common patterns of failure with multiple indications, additional testing may

There are many things that experienced tree risk assessors look for in assessing the structure of a tree. In this image, the fungal conks, extensive callus formation where branches have decayed and the cracked bark at the trunk bifurcation are certain signs that this hackberry trunk is about to fail. It is also important to note there is a large poison ivy vine with many protruding leaves sticking out that would pose poison ivy exposure to anyone removing this tree. It would be important to note this in the evaluation so that an arborist might take precautions.

be warranted. Sometimes the recommended abatement procedure is less costly than the testing procedure; therefore, it may be advisable to skip testing and go directly to abatement. There are many factors to look for when performing a Tree Hazard Evaluation. The ISA recommends using a Tree Hazard Evaluation Form to determine the relative risk of a tree in a group of trees and most arborists use this form when performing a tree hazard evaluation for tree owners and managers. The form includes information about tree characteristics, health, site conditions, targets, tree defects, hazard rating and comments. This information is critical in determining the hazard potential of a tree and is very useful in communicating risk levels to tree owners and managers.

Hazardous trees can have negative value because they are a liability until they are safely removed. This dead tree should have been removed long ago. This particular site had several trees that were threatening the neighboring development.

The plant appraiser must identify specific defects that increase the likelihood of failure hazard and the plant appraiser must decide the plant characteristics (present or absent) that are associated with non-failure. Appraisers must look for other specific features that are predictive of a potential failure, the presence or absence of which increase or decrease the likelihood of a tree failure and they may also be called upon to make estimations of safety as they pertain to the appraisal problem. Appraisers must also be able to apply weighted depreciation obsolescence for potential risk when it is warranted.

Risk Assessment

Risk Assessment is the systematic process of:

- evaluating what consequential things could happen,
- estimating how likely and under what constraints they are likely to occur, and
- communicating what the likely outcomes might be.

In tree management, it is the systematic process to determine the relative level of risk posed by a tree, tree part, or group of trees.

Tree Risk Assessment, according to ANSI A300 (Part 9), begins with the assignment type, definition and scope, which determine the extent and level of inspection. Assessment begins with identifying any targets and their occupancy rates. Next comes a description of the consequences of the tree or tree part impacting the target. This is followed by categorizing the risk into general groups of likelihood of failure, likelihood of impact, consequences of impact, the risk rating, or the risk reasonability threshold test. Next, the risk reasonability threshold gap is described in detail and recommendations are developed to bring the risk to a conformity standard or to an acceptable level of risk.

It is also important to consider the part size that could potentially fail. Larger and taller tree parts have a greater potential energy than do smaller, lower tree parts. Targets may have little value with the potential for total loss or they may be of great value with only moderate potential for partial loss. Depending on the size of the potential loss, consequences of impact due to a failure may be broadly categorized as negligible, minor, significant, or severe. Typically, risk assessment consequence is expressed in terms of monetary loss. In evaluating the meaningful potential for the tree to fail, an arborist must consider the likelihood that a particular tree part will fail over a window of time.

Tree risk assessment task is fraught with uncertainty as described earlier, but careful observation of a large number of tree risk characteristics and failure patterns (including the species, growth **habits**, branch attachments, tree defects, condition of the root system, uncompensated lean and the history of the tree) offers experienced tree risk assessors the best means to develop what I call "a snapshot of potential failure." It is a glimpse of what might happen under specific circumstances. This is a "best guess" and it is the best, most reliable opinion that professional tree risk assessors can offer today.

Because of the inherent uncertainty and unknowables involved, it is particularly difficult to accurately calculate specific numerical probabilities of failure from observations or research alone and the ANSI A300 (Part 9) does not dictate that probabilities of failure be reported as such. Since it is the best that we can offer, a best guess is appropriate to the scope of most professional plant appraisal assignments and the PA need not estimate risk to A300 standards, so long as high uncertainty of risk is disclosed as a condition of the appraisal. When calculating risk falls outside appraisal scope of work, that assignment condition should be clearly stated.

Trees often produce aesthetic and functional benefits that outweigh the risks of failure as perceived by their owners and no two arborists have the same level of experience, knowledge, training, judgment and competence to perform tree risk assessment tasks. Because of the unique challenges associated with tree risk assessment, two or three competent tree risk assessors may assess the same tree and arrive at very divergent tree risk assessment opinions, none of which have great certainty.

The very best that arborists can do is be vigilant in identifying those factors that could lead to tree failures and make the best recommendations possible, given the arborist's training, experience and judgment, with regard to the recognized patterns of tree failures. It is also important to communicate the limitations of predicting tree failures to tree owners and managers. The facts remain that, at some point, all trees have the potential to fail, and will fail if given enough time. The truth is that some trees will fail unpredictably and that there are profound limitations to the systematic risk assessment of trees. It is also important to understand that some tree failures that cause damage to property and/or injury or death to people are preventable and that such occurrences are infrequent. The

Trees like this Bradford pear are prone to sudden breakage. In a children's play area, the risk of a potential failure combined with the frequency of occupancy and the enormous liability the tree poses far outweighs any benefits that the tree might be producing.

worldwide chances of being struck by a tree are very similar to those of being struck by lightning, a very rare event. The difference is that sometimes tree impacts to targets are preventable through tree risk management and tree risk assessments. The consequences of impacts can sometimes be avoided by reducing the risk to people and property.

Risk Abatement

Risk abatement should always be a component of risk management when abatement is warranted. If a hazard has been determined to be at a level of risk higher than is acceptable to the tree owner or manager, the risk must be dealt with in such a way that the potential risk is reduced to an acceptable level. Sometimes this involves removal of the affected tree or part, but at other times, the treatment of the hazard may mean that a structural support system should be installed. Management may also mean removal of the target or restricting occupancy.

Often, the best option for lowering risk is pruning to either remove the defective part or reduce the weight of the branch above/beyond the defective part. Risk of failure cannot be eliminated completely without removal of the entire tree or targets. Also, trees tend to grow in ways that promote strong structure, so as the tree increases in size, their strength or their risk potential may increase. Sometimes, the best way to make a tree stronger is to perform treatments that increase their vigor and health. The more vigorous and healthy a tree is, the more capable it is of naturally adding strong healthy wood structure.

Risk abatement is usually not a one-time occurrence unless the questionable tree is removed. Whenever trees are being managed on a common property, on a non-rural private property, on a public site, or within a municipality, they should be evaluated on a periodic cycle that considers their size, age, overall condition and management practices.

In most common law jurisdictions, when a neighbor's tree limb hangs over an adjoining landowner's property, the adjoining owner has an absolute right to self-help and may, without permission, cut the intruding tree limbs off, up to the property line, and this right extends indefinitely upward. The neighbor on whose property the protruding limbs exist has exclusive rights above the land and those rights are protected from invasion by adjoining landowners to the same extent as surface rights. However, the absolute right of self-help removal of a tree limb encroachment is limited to limbs and not the trunk and is also limited to that which interferes with normal and reasonable land use or defective limbs and not necessarily any and all limbs that encroach since the indiscriminate removal of any and all limbs may be detrimental to someone else's tree that is not a nuisance.

Also, the neighbor acting upon his right of self-help may not permanently and unreasonably injure the neighbor's tree by trespass or by act of self-help negligence without liability of damages. In certain circumstances, trees near a boundary may be considered boundary trees with ownership as "tenants in common" where the acquiescence of the property owners has resulted in the trees becoming a partition between the properties. In such a situation, no action is permitted to be destructive or injurious to a tree that might impinge on the rights and benefits of either common owner.

While some property owners in some jurisdictions can be held responsible for damage to a neighbor's property that results from failing to attend to a tree that poses a threat, falling leaves don't fall into that category. According to English common law, falling leaves are considered a natural product of trees and not something for which the owner of the tree can be held liable. Homeowners, whether they own the tree or simply live next to it, are responsible for the cleanup of natural debris that alights to their property, no matter the source. The same holds true for tree sap, insect feces or any other tree droppings that do not result from human agency.

In the majority of jurisdictions, boundary trees are owned as "tenants in common," meaning that boundary trees are co-jointly owned and that common tenants of common trees must agree on any treatment that may be destructive. Depending on the fact patterns of the case, this situation may affect an opinion of value.

This public park tree was structurally unsound and needed to be removed. The stump was carved out to create child's play feature and a new tulip tree (Lirodendron tulipifera) was planted.

In professional plant appraisal it may be necessary to determine if risk abatement is warranted under the governmental requirement of reasonable **duty of care** and, if so, the appraiser must be able to calculate the estimated cost of such abatement. When risk assessment is within the appraisal assignment scope of work and when (according to the risk assessment results) the risk must be abated, the cost of abatement is estimated, and plant appraisers applies the appropriate amount of weighted depreciation when calculating an opinion of plant value.

Right-of-Way Vegetation Management

Many properties are encumbered by easements that allow the easement contract holder to enter upon the land and remove vegetation for various purposes. Electric utility operators typically hold easements near transmission, distribution and service lines. These easements do not typically extend from a service line pole to the structure that is serviced. Since electric (and other utility operators) are mandated to keep power supplied to electric customers, the easement holders have broad authority to keep the lines free of vegetation and objects that may interfere with operations of the facility. While the authority to clear and manage vegetation is broad, it is not an unlimited authority to cut and prune trees recklessly. Each jurisdiction is a little different as to what extent it will allow easement holders to prune and manage vegetation and each easement holder has their own policies regarding vegetation management. The plant appraiser should be aware of the limits of right-of-way vegetation management and their potential effects on plant values. When trees are planted in locations where they will be affected by ROW vegetation management practices,

Left: A row of tulip trees lining a driveway before right-of-way vegetation management pruning. Right: The location of the tree trunks was just outside the easement, but the branches and limbs to the right of the trunks were not, resulting in severe disfigurement and obsolescence of the functional and aesthetic tree benefits.

the appraiser should be able to evaluate the degree to which management will affect subject plants and be capable of calculating and applying any warranted obsolescence in the opinion of value.

Boundary Trees

A boundary tree is one in which some part of the above ground portion of the tree's main stem or trunk intersects a property boundary. A boundary tree may also be established by the acquiescence of time and care of mutual owners where trees serve as a partition between properties, even if a tree's trunk and buttress fall entirely on one side of a boundary or the other. Boundary trees are said to be owned in common, which means all owners have equal rights about the whole tree and no one owner may take away the rights of the other(s) without consent. It is also true that, while the main stem of a boundary tree may belong to all, the branches, twigs and leaves may be pruned over their respective owner's property without consent, so long as it does no permanent injury to the tree. Neither neighbor may take any unilateral action on a boundary tree, which may be detrimental to the tree, as a whole, or to the owners' rights and privileges as a whole without the consent of the other owner(s).

This can be a somewhat confusing issue for the plant appraiser because it is the purview of the court to decide some of these issues and it is the purview of attorneys to interpret the law when they serve as council or give legal advice. Nonetheless, plant appraisers must interpret the governmental forces that affect plant values and some of those forces are established statutorily by legislatures, some of those are established as case law from the bench and some are unknown and must be opined upon by the appraiser with advice from council. The plant appraiser should familiarize him/herself with the local law and regulation facts regarding trees and he/she should interpret those laws, regulations and their relevance as they pertain to the plant appraisal assignment. The plant appraiser must be able to defend their opinions, even to the court sometimes. While the court may divide a tree value in any way that is customary, parsing the tree's ownership between owners is the purview of the court and not the appraiser. The appraiser's function in such situations it to form an opinion of value on the entire tree.

Functional Limitations

With the advent of the Hawaii Rule governing more and more jurisdictions, tree owners often have some responsibility to maintain their own trees to prevent actual damage or the imminent threat of harm to their neighbors. With new responsibility comes new rights. While this is a relatively recent refinement to the old Massachusetts Rule, plant appraisers should be aware of both the benefits that trees produce to their owner and appraisers need to be aware of when trees and landscaping are a liability to their neighbor. Since all matters of law are the purview of lawyers and the courts, it is always a good idea to get a lawyer's opinion on legal status and matters of any legal case.

This champion ash tree is now threatened by emerald ash borer. This has a negative effect on value because the tree will need to be continually treated to prevent its demise and there are no guarantees that the tree will survive the plague.

CHAPTER TEN

ANALYSIS

THE OPINION OF PLANT APPRAISERS MUST NOT BE A SIMPLE matter of calculating a rudimentary formula. Analysis, in plant appraisal, involves a thorough understanding of each relevant characteristic and the benefits that those characteristics deliver to the user. Analysis involves judgments of how well those benefits are delivered/perceived. The benefits that amenity plants and landscaping can deliver (that may be anticipated by their owner) are either tangible (like the reduction in cooling costs that the shade of tree has on a building) or intangible (like the enjoyment one gets from seeing birds and other wildlife because of the habitat that a tree provides).

Historically, various amenity plant appraisal approaches and methods have been used to economically model the various benefits that amenity trees produce, but little has been done to explain what the benefits are and how to evaluate them. So far, the thrust of this book has been to assist PAs in identifying the relevant characteristics of amenity plants and in identifying the benefits that are produced as a result of those characteristics. There has also been a modest effort to explain how to judge the effectiveness in a plant's ability to deliver on those benefits in terms of depreciation.

Before we delve into the process of analyzing the data that is collected, it may be helpful to look at how this process has been done in the past so that we can better understand the logical refinements in amenity plant appraisal analysis that are presented hereafter.

CTLA

The Council of Tree and Landscape Appraisers (CTLA 2000) is a secretive organization that consists of a seven-member consortium with seven appointed individuals serving as representatives and seven alternates, representing seven key green industry associations. Those organizations are the American Nursery and Landscape Association (**ANLA**), the American Society of Consulting Arborists (**ASCA**), the American Society of Landscape Architects (**ASLA**), the Association of Consulting Foresters of America (**ACFA**), the National Association of Landscape Professionals (**NALP**) *(NALP was formerly known as the Associated Landscape Contractors of America (ALCA), the Professional Lawn Care Association of America (PLCAA) and the Professional Land Care Network (PLANET))*, the International Society of Arboriculture (**ISA**) and the Tree Care Industry Association (**TCIA**) *(TCIA was formerly the National Arborist Association — NAA)*. Together these seven associations represent approximately 350,000 green industry professionals who are involved in the planning, propagating, planting, maintenance and timber harvesting of trees in the United States. As CTLA representatives, each committee member solicits input from their respective constituency. Together, these seven individuals draft a document called the *Guide for Plant Appraisal*. Over the years, the Council has adopted many revisions and they are about to release a new edition. The 9th edition is the current guide in use at the publication of this book. (CTLA, 2000)

CTLA Guide for Plant Appraisal

The guide briefly describes the types of value that amenity trees and plants have and it describes several methodologies and processes involved with performing various types of PALs. This includes the **Trunk Formula Method**.

ASIDE: [***Uniform Standards of Professional Appraisal Practice (USPAP)*** offers some guidance with regards to identifying the appraisal problem and offers limited guidance as to the proper practice and procedures that PAs should follow when developing credible and reliable opinions of value. Of particular importance are the ethical standards of impartiality, the ethical standards of credibility and the other applicable standards of ethics that are expected of all PAs. The USPAP is also applicable in the identification of the appraisal problem's relevant characteristics and credible analysis of the relevant data that is collected when calculating appraisal results. (CTLA, 2000) (Appraisal Standards Board, 2015)]

Each professional plant appraisal assignment is governed by the type and definition of value that is sought and each assignment is constrained by the scope of work that is permitted by the minimum needs of the assignment and the maximum budget of the client. The assignment scope limits the extent to which data is gathered and limits are imposed by both the appraiser and the client based on their needs. Cost approach to value is common in plant appraisals that are not income approach. Since the PA is an authoritative expert on the relevant characteristics that produce the benefits of trees, is familiar with the costs of landscape contracting and is an expert on how the relevant characteristics would be used by plant owners, the scope of most PALs is usually limited to cost approach or income approach. Market approach is usually not possible with trees and landscaping since the relevant sales comparative data points for tree size, conditions, location and species are not locally and currently available.

Approaches to Value

Earlier, I said that there is no right value or wrong value; there is only value to whom or an opinion of value based on the relevant characteristics and the relevant data that corresponds to those characteristics. While this is true, there are also various ways to calculate value to whom, based on the processes by which those characteristics are observed, tested and analyzed. There are three generally recognized approaches of perception when it comes to appraised value opinions. Each approach represents a type of value or economic model that is derived from different kinds of relevant characteristics and their corresponding economic data.

Each approach answers a specific kind of question about worth. That question is, "What are the benefits that are sought and how are they anticipated?" In appraisal terms, we call these basic opinions about economic models the three approaches to value. The first and most important approach to value, when it comes to plants, is marked by the costs to produce or replace them. There may be a ready market venue for plants in exchange for money and that market data may be relevant to the wholesale or retail components of the appraisal problem, but that is only one of the cost inputs to putting a landscape into someone's yard. There are also design, transportation, labor, maintenance, and insurance costs. If a subject plant is not market available or if the data for the subject plant cannot be distilled from the real estate market transactions that are available, then a surrogate plant may need to be produced at a depreciated cost as a substitute for a readily-available market tree.

Because the costs or production/construction inputs are the basis of the opinion of value, regardless of market venue, this approach is called the cost approach. Cost is often the appraisal approach that is used in financing for commercial land development or for financing speculation construction of residential homes. For a variety of practical reasons, this is also the most commonly used approach in amenity tree and landscape appraisal. Cost approach is also very handy when appraising the value of something that has both tangible and intangible benefits that are anticipated in the specific ownership rights in that thing.

The next most important approach to value of amenity plants is income approach, which is based upon future earning potential and the likely returns that one would expect to enjoy over time as an investor might expect in the purchase of a thing, like an equity stake in a company or the purchase of income real estate. Appropriately enough, this approach to value is called the income approach.

The last and least applicable approach to professional plant appraisal is the comparative sales approach or market approach to value. This approach relies entirely on data that is derived from actual real estate market sales transactions (bid/ask pricing) when an "apples to apples" comparison is made between various relevant characteristics of like pairs of real estate improvements. The specific data used in such comparisons are extensively analyzed by REAs from every market segment to calculate value. In residential real estate appraisal, some of the more important data points include things like square footage of the land and structure, the age of the structure, style of the structure, structural component depreciation and many others. These vast data points are carefully examined and recorded by REAs for each appraisal assignment they perform, and the data points are stored in vast data bureau libraries for use in future appraisals. These data points are available to all REAs in each of their respective real estate markets.

While there are extensive real estate comparative sales data points, there are also many financial applications for their use, especially in mortgage lending. The comparative sales data points collected and analyzed by REAs are extensive, but they are not exhaustive. One notable area of data that is not captured or examined in the typical residential real estate market transaction is the value that trees and landscaping contribute to the real estate market price or landscape CREMV. While most real estate market participants (including buyers, sellers, brokers and appraisers) acknowledge that trees and landscaping play a critically important and potent role in real estate sales (much more important than an aside or noteworthy one) and in the desirability of real estate, this point of qualitative fact is not well quantified by REAs in practice. In reality, trees and landscaping are not quantified or evaluated in any meaningful way by the real estate appraisal community according to their own standard practices or procedures. The market scarcity and overall contribution to the sales price of an individual property by amenity plants is one aspect of real estate appraisal that the real estate market has completely abandoned. The collection of data regarding this specialized area of land improvement is missing from real estate data bureau data banks. Thus, the need for specialty amenity tree and landscape appraisal has grown and developed over the years. These important improvement land elements are typically treated as dirt by the real estate appraisal industry because it is not required that REAs understand how or even know why there would be a need to calculate landscape value for things like government-backed mortgages, which are the main purpose for most real estate appraisals.

The reason for this lack of understanding of landscape value by REAs is partly due to the complexity involved in performing plant appraisals and partly because there is a large gap in our understanding of the various pools of market participant behaviors regarding trees and landscaping. The level of competence that is required of most REAs is usually limited to that of land (dirt), structures, a few other improvements, income properties, or some other specialty appraisal practice. Most REAs are simply not equipped to competently quantify or qualify the appreciable and relevant function/amenity characteristics and benefits that trees and landscaping produce and that owners, sellers and buyers anticipate over time. Since some amenity characteristics of plants produce intangible benefits and since many of the tangible benefits are not quantified at all in the real estate sales market data, cost is nearly always the only means to credibly and reliably calculate the value of those benefits.

REAs simply have no credible basis for determining what role trees and landscaping play as CREMV over time! Challenges to the development of credible comparative analysis between various tree and landscape improvements are, in realty, immense and often require enormous efforts that would surpass all reasonable SOW of the REA assignment. Even if such efforts were undertaken, it could only bring about unreliable and incredible appraisal results. Accordingly, most REAs who need such inputs to fulfill tree and landscaping CREMV type assignments will delegate such questions to the vast education, training, experience and judgments possessed by specialty amenity plant appraisers. PAs are intimately familiar with the costs to produce the benefits that owners anticipate and enjoy because of landscaping. In a situation where landscaping must be appraised, the most relevant data that is available to the PA is very similar to the appraisal approach used by REAs in speculation home building or commercial investment. It is cost approach that is most reliable, credible and widely used, not market approach. The difference between new construction of a home and homes that have been in existence for many years is that, while homes typically deteriorate and depreciate over time (depending on maintenance and updating), landscape plants tend to grow bigger and appreciate over time.

GPA9's Four Cost Methods

Four GPA9 Cost Approach methods are available to the PA. They are **Cost of Cure**, **Cost of Repair**, **Replacement Cost** and **Trunk Formula Method**. Depending on the identification of the other appraisal problem elements, the fact patterns of the assignment and the SOW limitations, one or more cost methods or techniques may be used to calculate value.

GPA9's Cost of Cure Method

In GPA9, when extensive damage has occurred, it may not be possible to restore a site to its pre-damaged state. In such cases, returning a property to a reasonable approximation of its pre-damaged condition using variables in size, conditions, species and location (to replace the delivery of functional and aesthetic amenity tree benefits) is known as Cost of Cure Method. When site topography or ancillary features of a site play a role in landscape value, it may be most appropriate to cure the site rather than replace the individual trees or landscape parts. CTLA Cost of Cure Method is most appropriate in assignments when a site is cured by placing superior quality and species of smaller trees in superior locations. The same level and quality of benefits are delivered in the cure as was delivered by the subject(s). The aim of Cost of Cure plant replacement is the new establishment of benefits at the same level as the subject at the time of planting new. In the future, the new planting may deliver more benefits than the subject on the effective date of the appraisal. (United States v Lorance)

GPA9 Cost of Repair Method

Cost of Repair in GPA9 is well described; any refinements to it are beyond the scope of this book. See Cost of Repair in Chapter 11.

GPA9 Replacement Cost Method

GPA9 **Replacement Cost Method** can be used when damaged trees are of a commonly available, easily transportable and easily transplantable size. Size-for-size trees are replaced new and depreciated for species, location and condition of the subject.

GPA9 contains a suggested methodology for determining a plants condition. While this method may be suitable for preliminary appraisals that do not require much detail, it does not adequately address the need to account for the specific obsolescence in the delivery of specific benefits by specific plant parts. *It is the specific part of a plant that is responsible for delivery of specific benefits.* It is the physical ability of the individual plant part's benefit delivery system that should be weighed against the whole to obtain a credible depreciation result in the opinion of value. While some parts (like leaves and roots) are highly redundant, some parts (like the trunk) are not. The diminished ability of parts with high redundancies have less effect on benefit delivery than do diminishments of parts with low or no redundancies.

GPA9 Trunk Formula Method

GPA9 Trunk Formula Method is very similar to Replacement Cost Method and is used when the tree is very large and/or is not commonly available. GPA9 Trunk Formula Method has traditionally been used for subject trees that cannot be easily transported and/or easily transplanted or if sales/pricing data of subject tree species is not commonly or easily available. In this method, the appraised tree trunk is measured, and the area of the trunk calculated (and if large enough, it is potentially adjusted for size). Then, the largest commonly available nursery stock surrogate and landscape construction tree data is used to calculate costs to buy, transport, transplant, establish and guarantee a new tree.

In GPA9, cumulative obsolescence is calculated for species, condition and location. In GPA9, the Replacement Tree Cost is divided by the replacement tree trunk area to determine Unit Tree Cost. The calculation of unit tree costs is essential to establish a relationship of the size of a tree to the delivery of benefits. The surrogate tree is assumed to be of standard nursery stock and to be of high quality or 100% condition. The surrogate tree is also assumed to be placed ideally in the landscape for benefits delivery and is assumed to be growing in ideal site conditions. All the costs associated with the purchase, transport, transplant, establishment, maintenance and guarantee may (if SOW allows) be researched and analyzed for accuracy. The Installed Tree Cost is typically divided by its trunk area to derive unit cost. While trunk area is commonly used as the unit value, it is only one form of unit measure to benefits equivalency. **Canopy area** and canopy volume have also been effectively used as units of measure. Regardless of the unit used, the calculation of benefits delivered must be based on units that are the same in both the subject tree and the surrogate replacement. The Increased Trunk area of the appraised tree is then multiplied by the Unit Tree Cost and is added to the installed tree cost to determine Basic Tree Cost.

In Trunk Formula Method, the trunk area is analyzed as the benefits equivalency unit of measure. While this tree trunk has defects that may affect the area of the trunk's cross section, the character of the trunk also adds an important aesthetic to this landscape design.

In GPA9, the Basic Tree Cost is then depreciated by the subject trees' Species Rating, **Location Rating** and **Condition Rating** to arrive at Appraised Value, which is then rounded. Where GPA9 Trunk Formula Method falls short is in its ability to attribute the individual anticipated benefits to the relevant conditions and characteristics of the individual plant parts responsible for delivering on those benefits. As a refinement to GPA9, the appraiser may consider the suitability of the site conditions to the species that was selected and consider the effectiveness of plant placement in the delivery of benefits for each plant part. As you examine these factors closely, their effect on benefits delivery will become apparent in various ways. The appraiser uses qualified judgment to form an opinion as to the percentage of effectiveness of the plant part to deliver the anticipated benefit. Plant part conditions, species/site and species/placement all have influence on the value of plants to owners and should be weighed appropriately to establish credible and reliable appraisal depreciation results.

It is possible to follow guidance from the *CTLA Guide for Plant Appraisal Trunk Formula Method, 9th Edition* to appraise trees. However, another area where this guidance falls short is in the understanding of why amenity trees have value and how to apply depreciation based on the benefits produced by the various plant parts. While GPA9 does allow for a general depreciation for location, condition and species, GPA9 offers no guidance on how or why the various plant part conditions affect the specific delivery of benefits that trees can produce. Also, GPA9 suggests that appraisers consider various functional and aesthetic benefits in their estimating contribution ratings, but GPA9 makes no attempt to give guidance on how to analyze these specific benefits in terms of the relevant subject characteristics. Without this critical context, the analysis of plant species/placement within the site conditions, there can be no objective identification of delivery deficiencies and no assessment of plant benefits delivery effectiveness. The critical context of benefits delivery is made possible by identifying the condition of the plant part and by identification of deficiency due to plant part deterioration. Deterioration influences delivery of specific benefits. By identifying deficiencies in landscape placement characteristics, another aspect of obsolescence is identified and similarly judged deficient based on how effective the placement permits the plant or tree to deliver its benefits.

To objectively assess plant benefits individually, the plant appraiser must identify the plant species, the condition of the component plant parts, the plant's placement within the landscape and delivery effectiveness of each benefit being delivered. Once the plant appraiser has analyzed each component plant part for effective delivery of benefits, all benefits may be scaled for importance. The easiest way to do this is to assign an appropriate percentage of weight to each individual benefit with the total weight of all benefits equal to 100%. Weight for each benefit is applied as to its importance in the appraisal opinion. Attributes that deliver greater benefits to an owner should be given more weight than benefits that deliver less. The application of weight to benefits delivery is a little more subjective since no two appraisers have the same experience, education, training and ability to correctly identify deficiencies of design or ability to detect when proper design characteristics are absent. When deficiencies in delivery of benefits exist due to poor plant part conditions or plant placement or site conditions, the appraiser must account for those deficiencies as obsolescence. Appraisers with similar training, education and experience should be able to arrive as similar conclusions with regard to judging obsolescence.

CHAPTER ELEVEN

Cost Approach From a Real Estate Perspective

The challenge for PAs is that the relevant characteristics of the subject tree or landscaping (which are part of realty property as improvement elements) are not adequately or appropriately segregated or parsed in the comparative sales data sets that would typically be used in paired data sales analysis of landscaping and amenity trees. Also challenging is the establishment, tree unit costs (developed from the costs to buy, transport, transplant, maintain and guarantee nursery stock) as relevant to the benefits that landscape trees deliver to owners and prospective owners. Are the unit costs of the smaller replacement trees relative to those of a larger surrogate tree? According to past experiences of myself, other experienced arborists and the courts, there is a link between the unit cost of producing a smaller nursery tree and the exponentially larger costs of producing much larger trees. There is also an exponential increase in the production of plant benefits as the tree increases in size from a smaller nursery sized tree to a larger landscape sized subject tree. The benefits that trees deliver increase proportionally with tree size. The question becomes one of reconciliation between the appreciation of benefits that accrue over time as the smaller tree becomes larger and the greater amount of benefits that a tree of much larger size delivers. Since the real estate market does not provide us with the answers to that specific question, replacement cost and other cost methods, less obsolescence, must be relied upon to that end. This is the only credible way to solve residential and institutional PAL problems today.

The cost approach is necessary when reliable comparative sales or income data are absent. Cost is the approach that is most relied upon for valuing specialty properties like parks and government buildings or new construction. That is because there are usually few sales of comparable properties to inform a credible sales comparison approach to the appraisal result. Such specialty property is typically not identified by REAs when it comes to mortgages; moreover, these specialty properties are not generally itemized, even though they are sometimes used (either directly or indirectly) to generate income streams. Specialty real property improvements are almost always informed by cost approach; hence the name, specialty improvement. The cost approach to value involves estimating the cost of replacing the property new and subtracting any loss in value due to physical deterioration and other obsolescence in the delivery of benefits. The remainder after subtracting obsolescence is the estimate of cost type values. There are many situations where cost approach is the most reliable to inform an opinion of value and where cost is the most appropriate approach to solve an appraisal problem. (Ling D. C., 2008)

Cost approach is the most common approach to value in amenity plant appraisal. In this approach, a plant appraiser determines the cost to replace, repair, or cure trees and landscaping. This approach is most appropriate in situations where income approach and market approach are not appropriate or when other approaches do not accurately model the functional and aesthetic amenity tree benefits that are delivered by a tree and anticipated by users. (Internal Revnue Service, 2017)

In the cost approach to tree appraisal, the cost to repair, replace, produce or cure the functional and aesthetic amenity tree benefits is the basis of value. This type of PAL is very similar to cost-type appraisals of other properties, such as costs to cure, produce or replace real estate improvements that are not parsed and captured in the comparative sales data that is typically used for government-backed mortgages. In damage cases, the plant appraiser considers (in detail) the size, species, location and condition of the trees that were damaged or cut and the appraiser calculates the cost to buy, install and **establish** size, species and condition tree(s) in the same location to produce the same benefits that were lost. In circumstances where trees are larger than are commercially available, the plant appraiser selects unit cost method and finds large commercially available nursery stock tree(s) and the costs to transport, transplant, etc. Adjustments can be made to reach parity with the subject of the appraisal. Cost approach is the most appropriate in cases where there is ample data available to calculate the cost to replace the functional and aesthetic benefits that a tree produces. (CTLA, 2000) (Internal Revnue Service, 2017)

The cost approach can be a very useful, credible and reliable method of determining an opinion of value for special kinds of property. Properties that have unique characteristics and/or have no sales data sets from which to draw comparative sales analysis judgments can be valued based on the the basis of cost to produce the anticipated benefits.

The SOW involved in cost approach may be minimal or it may be extensive and detailed, depending on what is needed to fulfill the assignment. Of course, there is the potential that the cost to build a thing will not fetch the same amount of sales revenue in the marketplace for a variety of reasons and sometimes that relationship cannot be known due to the special characteristics that are relevant to the appraisal problem. In amenity tree and landscape CREMV assignments, REAs must reconcile the cost values to the factors that influence market conditions and the REA must determine what the amenity tree and landscape CREMV is in the overall sales transaction, an impossible problem to solve when no data for such CREMV exists. Fortunately, there is very little need for amenity tree and landscape CREMV in the real estate markets. Even when it is called for under special circumstances, there are reasonable techniques for dealing with amenity trees and landscaping as standalone elements at cost, thus removing the need for sales comparisons of landscape and tree improvements to the land. This practice has been thoroughly tested and proven at the highest levels.

When developing the cost approach to value there are three basic types that can be sought. First, the value that is sought is the cost to produce new, minus the depreciation that the old one contained at the effective date. That is the production costs of labor, materials, transportation, guarantees, other expenses, plus profit new, then subtracting from that new thing, any deficiencies that the preexisting thing had just before the time when the thing was damaged or lost. The value of these deficiencies are what is known as obsolescence and the analysis of obsolescence results in a depreciation deduction from value.

The second type of cost is called reproduction cost. Reproduction cost is (by Appraisal Institute definition) the cost to put it back exactly the way it was, including any deficiencies or obsolescence that the preexisting thing contained just before it was damaged or lost. In this type of appraised value, there is no depreciation because the reproduction of the thing contains all deficiencies that the original had.

NOTE: It is important to note here that, for simplification in this book, the definition of reproduction is a narrow one. The insurance industry, the federal government and other entities may define reproduction differently; thus, a different type and definition of value with appropriately differing assignment procedures may apply.

The third type of cost value is called functional replacement (not to be confused with the functional benefits of trees. Here, functional refers to all benefits that a tree produces). In this type of cost value, the exact functional and aesthetic benefits are calculated and thoroughly analyzed. Once the benefits are known, the appraiser develops a plan to recreate those benefits as closely as possible to the original, using different plant species, size, placement and/or conditions.

While each of these types of cost have advantages for a given situation, it may be appropriate for the appraiser to communicate with the client on the advantages and disadvantages of using one type and definition of value over another. Most of the time, however, one type of cost appraisal will be most appropriate to a given appraisal problem. Occasionally, more than one cost method will be used to determine a range of values for the most reasonable solution to the appraisal problem.

Subject Size v Replacement or Surrogate or Multiple Variable Cure

In its simplest form, cost approach directly replaces the subject tree(s) species for species, size-for-size, in the exact same location. The cost to buy, to transport, to transplant, to maintain the tree to establishment and to guarantee the tree's establishment in the site are tabulated and obsolescence for physical deterioration is applied. This is called Direct Replacement Method (DRM).

Nursery-sized trees like this one that are commonly available can be replaced size-for-size. Larger trees that have been growing for some time (like the one in the background) are not easily transported or transplanted and cannot be easily replaced size-for-size.

Sometimes subject plants and particularly subject trees, often grow to very great size near to structures or other obstacles in such a way that it is difficult or impossible to successfully harvest and transplant a new tree size-for-size. Likewise, it is often not possible nor practical to successfully harvest a large replacement tree, move it and transplant it to a site where severe space limitations or limitation in topography exist. In replacement appraisal problems with these types of parameters, the solution may be obtained by using a surrogate tree of commonly available size and species of new condition that is suitable for transplanting to the site. While it may be nearly impossible for a similar subject-sized tree to be planted in the exact same location, it may be much easier to grow a tree from a smaller size and adapt it to the site conditions (as the subject tree had originally grown).

While larger trees can be successfully transplanted, there are proper standards for executing such work. This tree's branch structure and root ball size did not conform to ANSI Z60 standards for nursery stock and it did not conform to ANSI A300 (Part 6) for planting as it was planted about eight inches too deep and was being overwatered. The guying material was also installed improperly.

One way to analyze the cost of growing a new tree is to find the unit cost of buying, transporting, transplanting, maintaining to establishment and guaranteeing establishment of a smaller surrogate tree, and applying the unit cost of the smaller tree to the larger tree and then deduct for depreciated obsolescence. This is called Unit Cost Method.

Another way to measure the cost of growing a new tree is to calculate all the inputs that are needed to grow a smaller replacement tree to an equivalent size of the subject tree in the exact same location as the subject and depreciating for obsolescence. As with the Unit Formula Method, the cost of buying, transporting, transplanting, maintaining to establishment and guaranteeing establishment of a smaller surrogate tree is tabulated. But instead of developing a unit cost, the appraiser calculates the time and cultural inputs that are needed to grow the smaller tree to an equivalent subject size. Time is used to calculate the costs of cultural care inputs that are needed to reach tree size parity and, if applicable, time may be used to measure the benefit stream gap that occurs between a small tree's supply of benefits and a larger subject trees delivery of benefits. These costs are depreciated for obsolescence to calculate value. This cost technique is called the Time Cost Method.

Another option the appraiser may use to solve this type of problem is to change the location of the size-for-size replacement tree to another area of the site where the size-for-size replacement tree will deliver the same level of benefits. Furthermore, an appraiser may choose to use many new, smaller trees of greater quality of different species delivering greater functional and aesthetic benefits in more locations to effectively deliver the same amount and type of benefits that are delivered by the single subject tree. In multiple variable solutions to cost, depreciation is applied as a deduction in the number of trees needed to fulfill the benefits delivered. In this multiple variable type of appraisal scenario, the curative trees start out delivering the same level of benefit that the subject delivered, but these substitute trees may (post effective date) increase the benefits they deliver, in time, over those delivered by the subject. In fact, the new benefits delivered may be far greater than that delivered by the subject tree well into the future after successful transplanting takes place. This option is called Cost to Cure Method.

While each cost method offers credibility and reliability advantages to solving the cost approach problems, the body of authority (the body that makes the final decisions about which cost method is allowable and which ones are not) will have jurisdiction. The answer to the question of when each method is most appropriate may be determined by the jurisdictional authority as a matter of law over how cost data are accumulated, calculated and processed within the appraisal problem. Governance over how cost methods are most appropriately to be applied may be wide and varied. As bodies of authority and as PAs become more familiar with the various cost methods, more clarity on their governance and use will surely follow. It is incumbent upon plant appraisers to become familiar with the governance of plant appraisals within the local jurisdiction of the property where they perform plant appraisals.

Replacement Cost New Calculations

Like other cost appraisal of improvements to land, old trees and landscaping are usually replaced new and depreciated for obsolescence. With trees and shrubs, replacement cost is always replacement *new* as of the effective date as opposed to original, historical or book cost. Also, there is an ethics issue with arborists intentionally using substandard trees and plants, or with arborists recommending use of obsolescent trees and shrubs to intentionally create obsolescence in physical deterioration That is because these activities are performed under ANSI A300 and work performed short of these standards may be perceived as arboricultural malpractice. While it is possible to create substandard specifications to build obsolescence into an appraisal problem, who could be employed to implement them? Certainly not a competent arborist.

The size of trees and shrubs is a critical consideration when calculating replacement new. While nursery trees come in a variety of sizes that are readily available in the contract construction of landscaping, subject trees in the landscape are often larger than the replacement nursery stock. While it is possible to transport, transplant, maintain and guarantee very large trees in a variety of situations, it is not always practical to estimate and calculate those costs within professional plant appraisal scopes of work. Professional plant appraisal tools and techniques have been developed to assist the PA in the formulation of ethical, reliable and credible opinions of value for larger trees and plants based on the unit cost of readily available nursery stocks.

If the subject tree or shrub is of commonly available nursery stock size, there is no need to develop unit cost benefit equivalency and the replacement new is direct. Depreciation is similarly applied in both Replacement Cost New (tree for tree) and in Unit Formula Method (tree for tree surrogate).

When calculating Replacement Cost New, the appraiser must identify the exact physical condition of the subject on the effective date, identify any functional obsolescence that exists and identify how much aesthetic obsolescence exists.

The existing subject plant's physical condition is compared to the condition of the replacement and deprecation is typically calculated for physical deterioration in terms of percentage. Physical deterioration occurs for each plant part that is responsible for the delivery of specific benefits. The functional and aesthetic obsolescence are a measure of the diminishment in 1) the delivery of benefits due to the physical ability of species limited by the site characteristics, and 2) the delivery of functional and aesthetic benefits intended in the selection and placement of species in the landscape design.

Obsolescence may also be calculated in terms of the difference in species or variety between the subject and the replacement. Sometimes there is no species difference between the replacement and the subject, sometimes the replacement species is superior in some way to the subject and sometimes the replacement is deficient to the subject in some way. The appraiser must determine any differences in species that exist between the replacement and the subject and determine what that will mean in terms of appreciable/depreciable benefits to the owner, expressed as a percentage. Similarly, the location or external placement of trees and landscaping can improve the appreciable benefits that the tree or landscaping can provide when the replacement reaches maturity. While depreciation is normally applied as a percentage that negatively affects value in Replacement Cost New method, depreciation in Cost to Cure is handled quite differently.

Quantitative Functional Analysis

The functional benefits that amenity plants produce is identified as relevant and may be capable of delivering most of their benefits efficiently to an anticipating owner. If there are deficiencies in the delivery of functional benefits, the appraiser will apply an obsolescence deduction that is appropriate to the deficiency.

Qualitative Landscape Analysis

This part of the analysis for obsolescence requires knowledge of landscape design. The questions in **"Qualitative Assessment of Landscape Design", Appendix A-3,** can be helpful in deciding how much depreciation to apply for poor quality or deficiencies in design.

There are templates for calculating unit cost, depreciation and a spreadsheet that contains many of the calculations you will need is available at http://www.ProAPAH.com/forms. Click on the form you need and enter the code: ProForms.

Once the aesthetic benefit deficiencies are identified, the appraiser considers how well each plant part delivers on the aesthetic benefits that each plant part produces and how well the plant owner should anticipate receiving those benefits from the plant part. Typically, each plant part will be rated 10% to 90% on aesthetic benefits delivery. Use the model

Ancillary features like this inviting bench serve a variety of both functional and aesthetic uses.

for weighing benefits that are anticipated and the benefit obsolescence of both functional and aesthetic use.

Landscape Use Obsolescence

This category of obsolescence deals with the fundamental way in which the plant is suited to its selection and placement in the site for its intended landscape use. On the surface, this can seem to be a more subjective type of obsolescence to the uninformed observer, but when carefully examined and analyzed, this type of obsolescence requires the same level of skill and experience as the professional judgments of a plant's physical conditions. To calculate landscape use obsolescence, the PA should examine the perceived or intended landscape benefits that the plant produces, the suitability of the plant species to that use and any limits to the perceived or intended benefits produced. Landscape use obsolescence is the limitation that the plant's location within the landscape places on the plant's ability to fully deliver its perceived or intended benefits.

Physical Deterioration or Condition - Species/Site/Condition = Internal Obsolescence

In real estate appraisal, physical deterioration is normally the physical wear and tear that begins when the construction of a structure is completed and put into service. As structures age through use, time and the elements, they will eventually wear out and eventually fall into disrepair. Typically, this requires additional work to bring a structure to a like-new condition. Similarly, trees may develop defects, such as decay, or may grow poorly or may even develop dangerous physical structures. These defective physical attributes in trees and landscaping are observed, measured and evaluated as part of the depreciated cost analysis. In addition to the physical defects that may be observed, trees and other plants are unique among realty improvements in that they are living organisms and are capable not only of increasing in size over time (which increases the benefits they provide), but they also are sometimes capable of outgrowing their structural defects. The PA makes observations about the physical conditions of the various plant parts and judges their conditions according to the tree's ability to sustainably and effectively deliver their associated benefits.

The fungal conks on this branch are positive indication of decay, which is also physical deterioration obsolescence in branches.

Because plants are living organisms, they can have defects in both anatomical structure characteristics (and structures can be evaluated based on the quality of the component structure) and they have health characteristics (which may be evaluated on the basis of overall vitality and vigor of the plant). While some trees may be anatomically strong, trees can also be in a weakened state health-wise. Disease, insects, environmental stress and genetic makeup all play a role in a tree's health condition. The symptoms that weakened trees exhibit can have profoundly negative effects on the benefits that tree provides.

Appreciation/Depreciation Calculations

Living trees and shrubs in landscaping are unique among all land improvements in that they tend to get larger over time. Their increased size tends to create greater benefits to their owner over time. This makes older larger plants more valuable and this value increases exponentially as time passes. At some point, however, larger, older trees will no longer command increased sales quantities at the nursery. Nursery trees will command a minimal price for smaller seedlings, **liners**, or bare rootstock. Accordingly, the unit price of such stock is exponentially smaller than is that of the larger market-ready stock. As the tree nursery stock approaches 1–10 inches **caliper**, the market demand peaks and (depending on the nursery model) most of the stock (by dollar volume of trees sold) is sold in this size range. As the nursery crop becomes depleted and the sales of ever increasing tree sizes grow beyond that of common harvest size and transportability, the demand for new, smaller nursery crops commands more nursery space occupied. The demand for a new crop begins to outweigh the larger sales prices of larger trees and the larger crop yields experience diminishing returns over field space. As the pool of large plant buyers decreases, the nursery profitability model for the same field space also diminishes. Nurseries plan for these crop size increases and diminishing returns in their business models and they cull depleted crop fields when more space is needed for a new, younger crop. Sometimes a nursery will sell out of a crop before more space is necessary and the planting of new, young stock comes earlier than planned.

Each plant part is responsible for delivering certain benefits. Some of the benefits that a plant delivers are functional and some of the benefits are aesthetic. In analyzing the benefits for obsolescence, the appraiser identifies the benefits that are produced and weighs these benefits against all of the other benefits that are being appraised. The appraiser judges the amount that individual benefit contributes among the entire bundle of benefits being delivered by the tree (that is, the percentage of single benefit among all benefits as a whole). This individual benefit is identified with the plant part that delivers it and it is depreciated for physical deterioration (which includes any site/species deficiencies) and is depreciated by deficiencies in landscape use placement. Each benefit is likewise identified and depreciated until 100% of the benefits are similarly analyzed for obsolescence. The resulting sum is deducted from the basic tree value.

See "Model of Cost Depreciation of Plants", Appendix A-4

Unit Formula Method Calculations

The unit cost method is applied to the appraisal problem when a subject tree is larger than commonly available and easily transportable nursery stock. Drawing from my own experience and the experience of other professional plant appraisal experts, the unit cost of harvesting, transporting, transplanting, maintaining and guaranteeing nursery-sized trees is very similar to the unit cost of harvesting, transporting, transplanting, maintaining and guaranteeing much larger trees.

There exists a factually-based assumption that the Unit Cost Method of plant appraisal will yield similar monetary values of the following:

- Growing a smaller replacement nursery tree in situ, to parity size of the subject (via cost inputs of maintenance over time) plus the size/benefit stream gap equals a tree for tree value, or
- Unit costs of a scaled surrogate replacement equals a tree-for-tree value, or
- Moving and establishing a large tree that is similar in size and species, to the subject equals tree value.

In previous editions of the CTLA guide, unit formula was called Trunk Formula Method. This method involved identification and calculation of costs to develop unit costs for the production of a surrogate Basic Tree Cost. To calculate Unit Tree Costs, local landscape construction costs (which are commonly available) of a Replacement New tree are analyzed and appropriated to produce a new tree, using a commonly available and easily transportable nursery stock tree. These costs include:

- Wholesale/retail nursery stock costs
- Transportation costs
- Labor costs
- Equipment and material costs to install the nursery stock
- Insurance/guarantee costs
- Plant establishment maintenance costs

Basic Tree Cost Calculation

Once the replacement tree new costs are calculated, they are divided by the square inch area of the trunk at caliper or standard height to find the unit cost of the of the new tree. This unit cost can be used to calculate the value of the surrogate basic tree cost. Multiplying the unit cost by the increased trunk area of the subject tree and adding the installed tree cost gives you the basic tree cost. This basic tree cost is then depreciated by the obsolescence contained in the benefits delivery depreciation analysis. Multiplying by the total depreciation percentage yields the appraised value.

While using the trunk area as the basis of benefit equivalency is sufficient for a broad range of plant appraisal assignments, there are both advantages and disadvantages to using the trunk. First, trunk measurements have been standardized and are widely used in both urban and forest environments. The data for these measurements is widely available and is commonly used among a variety of professional and scientific disciplines. In short, using the trunk as a measure of benefits equivalency is very convenient.

Trunk measure is limited in that the trunk is not the primary means of benefit delivery. Of all the plant parts, the leaves and canopy of trees are the primary means of delivery and since the canopy can be measured, it may make more sense to use a canopy measurement as the more relevant or more accurate means of communicating benefit equivalency. Also, sites with a very dense population of trees may have many trees in close proximity where the tree trunks are super adequate for the benefits that are produced. In such a situation, the cumulative canopy area of the tree stand would offer a more accurate measure of benefits equivalency. When unit cost method scenarios call for canopy instead of using trunk area of the nursery stock tree, the canopy area of the nursery stock tree is measured on both the subject and the stock and calculated using square canopy units instead of square units of trunk.

Whether using trunk measurement or canopy measurement, it is important to use the same unit of measure for both the subject that is being appraised and the replacement or surrogate tree. Also, canopy area data is readily available from public domain sources while volume data is more difficult to obtain and may require a site examination of both the subject and the nursery trees.

See "Unit Formula Appraised Value Worksheet", Appendix A-2.

Unit Formula Method Depreciation Calculations

In past editions of the CTLA guide, depreciation of the entire tree was calculated for species, location and physical condition. While the breakdown of these calculations offered some refinement in the calculation of obsolescence from prior plant appraisal work, the GPA9 process of calculating and applying obsolescence did not provide the appraiser with any means of directly applying deterioration to the individual plant parts responsible for delivery of benefits. In fact, GPA9 offers no means at all of isolating the individual benefits or their relative importance among those benefits being weighed in the calculation of value. For example, GPA9 condition rating for the entire tree was applied to all the benefits delivered by the whole tree and likewise to the species of the whole tree and its location.

In the improved Unit Formula Method, depreciation for obsolescence is applied as a refinement in judgments of deterioration in individual plant parts and as deficiency in the delivery of the weighted benefits that are supplied by those parts. Another aspect of refinement described in this book is the obsolescence that results from poor plant placement within the landscape design. Each plant part is evaluated for production of benefits and the landscape's aesthetic benefits are identified and judged for efficiency. Depreciation deductions are made where design placement results in a deficiency of maximum delivery of benefits.

Like Replacement Cost New, total depreciation is calculated as a percentage and is multiplied by the basic tree to find Appraised Value. The Appraised Value is rounded to the nearest $10.00 for Appraised Values under $5,000.00 and rounded to the nearest $100.00 for Appraised Value of $5,000.00 and over.

There are templates for calculating unit cost, depreciation and a spreadsheet that contains many of the calculations you will need available at http://www.ProAPAH.com/forms. Click on the form you need and enter the code: ProForms.

See table "Model of Cost Depreciation of Plants," Appendix A-4.

Cost to Cure Calculations

Cost to Cure methodology in plant appraisal is the cost to restore landscape improvements to a reasonable approximation of a pre-existing state of the anticipated benefits of the subject(s). This method comes into play when it is not possible to replace trees or substitute a replacement of the size and number of subject plants in the same placement as the subject being appraised. This technique is particularly useful in sites that have experienced excavation changes in topography and where pre-existing ancillary features are damaged or destroyed. Costs to Cure damage is calculated by estimating expenditures of all restorative efforts to bring the lost functional and aesthetic benefits of a site near to a reasoned approximation to the pre-existing state. Cost of Cure is primarily interested in curing a loss in functional and aesthetic benefits produced at the time of loss without attempting to replace the exact same size and species of plants, in their exact pre-existing locations. Aesthetic and functional benefits of pre-existing landscaping are calculated, and a redesign of the landscape is comprised of select plant species, plant sizes and plant placement to produce a reasoned approximation of pre-existing benefits. Since curative plants are assumed to be of superior quality, species and placement to maximize benefits delivery over pre-existing site conditions, parity is reached by:

- identifying the canopy size,
- identifying the relevant benefits delivered,
- identifying the deficiencies of the pre-existing landscape benefits delivery,
- applying those deficiencies as depreciated obsolescence to the canopy size,
- reducing the size of the replacement plants to what is commonly available,
- improving the quality of the curative plants,
- improving the species of the curative plants,
- improving the location of the curative plants,
- increasing the number of curative plants (if needed),
- identifying any remedial site treatments that will need to be employed,
- estimating costs, and
- calculating the costs.

Selecting improved replacement species and placing them in better locations for benefits delivery of the preexisting benefits in a more efficient package is the aim of Cost to Cure. In some instances, the loss of use in functional and aesthetic benefits cannot be fully cured at once due to space limitations. In such situations, it may be necessary to calculate a relationship of maintenance costs to time of parity (where restoration is fully realized). In such situations, the Cost to Cure may be added to maintenance costs over time to parity. The difference between curative costs and the time to benefits parity is called Supplementary Cost. If a tree or plant is a total loss, the cost of removal and cleanup may be added to the Cost to Cure the subject trees or plants to fully account for the costs. For a comprehensive list of Cost to Cure tasks, see GPA9 and the corresponding Cost of Cure Field Report Form Folder.

When performing Cost to Cure analysis, it is useful to develop a matrix of the various functional and aesthetic amenity benefits and how they were delivered by the quantities and sizes of pre-existing species. Most sites have historical imagery showing the size and location of tree canopies. Since it may not be possible to measure the trunk of pre-existing plants in a heavily manipulated or a destroyed site, it may be helpful to use pre-existing canopy area or volume as the benefits delivery unit equivalency rather than the trunk unit equivalency. When selecting new curative plants, they should be of size and species that are strategically placed in the landscape to maximize benefits delivery that, in time, may exceed the pre-existing benefits delivery. The delivery of benefits in the cure cost + supplementary costs = the delivery of depreciated benefits delivery in the subject as of the effective date of the appraisal.

Here is an example of Cost to Cure:

EXAMPLE

An eminent domain taking has resulted in the excavation of land and the loss of a stand of trees. The stand of trees is situated on a sloping hill that rises to a large residential structure in a rural setting with a prized view. Aerial photographs of the pre-existing trees were measured to calculate the two dimensional canopy area of the loss and a site visit examination yielded data from a similar plot of trees where the subject tree conditions, species and benefits were identified. Note that we are only concerned with the placement of the trees on the property as to how well the subject trees were able to deliver on the benefits to their owner.

Curative plant costs included prices and installation costs for benefits of trees, shrubs and or/groundcovers species and/or other vegetative species that had been damaged or destroyed. Labor costs for curative plants affected by re-vegetation **specifications** were estimated. These specifications included factors such as strict schedules, special planting guidelines, specific soil amendment requirements and other pertinent considerations.

Since the exact number, size, species, condition and location of trees lost was not known, aerial photographs of tree canopies

Site map shows canopy loss (in blue) due to installation of natural gas pipeline.

EXAMPLE

were used to determine unit size. This is a common practice when tree density creates superadequacy in the unit measure of tree trunks. Sample data from nearby tree stands was also used as surrogates to determine tree conditions and species ratings because the preexisting trees and stumps were destroyed. In this case, the canopy was measured and depreciated for species, condition and placement as obsolescence of canopy size equivalency of the benefits delivered. The largest commonly available, easily transportable, easily transplantable, high quality condition and species of nursery stock plants were then selected for superior aesthetic and species qualities to cure the benefits of the canopy that was lost to cutting. A landscape design was developed, and the curative trees were placed to optimize their functional and aesthetic characteristics.

Species characteristics and adaptability coupled with site condition (that is soil, exposure and slope) were serious considerations that had be thoroughly understood before the quantity and size of species used were designed into the cure. This ecological information also applied to the selection of alternative species to the subjects. Since young curative plants have an excellent potential for re-establishing a damaged site, they are much more cost efficient. However, while plants are becoming established, they may need special care. The highest loss rates on a damaged site are within the first year of planting. Most of these losses can be prevented by following establishment protocols that consider cultural, biological and/or chemical tasks.

EXAMPLE

This cure included a long list of restorative maintenance tasks including phases of:

- Proper irrigation
- Mulching
- **Root collar** protection
- Control of competitive vegetation
- Pruning
- Pest management
- Fertilization

The following considerations were useful in the development of cure specifications:

Applying water at the proper time, in the right location and in the proper amount is the most critical factor in the survival of curative vegetation. Water should be applied both within the original root zone and in the surrounding soil. Too little water and too much water are harmful to a curative plant. Moisture levels were properly monitored, so restorative tasks included installing tensiometers to measure soil moisture for specific plant needs.

Properly applied mulch conserves soil moisture and provides an environment for roots that is like forest duff. Root collar inspections should be done on all curative trees. When soil or mulch contacts the trunk, too much moisture can be held next to the bark, which may lead to **decline** and disease. Pruning at the time of planting should be limited to removal of dead, diseased, dying and broken limbs. During planting, however, minor structural pruning may be warranted. Corrective pruning may be a consideration in the future.

A large plant may be cured by estimating the number of plants it would take to cure its previous functional or aesthetic benefits. Using this provision, one should not overplant or under-plant. An appraiser's duty is to give special care, thought and attention to the amount and type of plants for curing benefits that were lost. Total Plant Cost may be adjusted by plant condition, location and species if subject plants exhibit a variance in health as compared to the new nursery curative plants. Plant adjustment includes analyzing the species, condition and location of trees prior to being damaged. An appraiser should be familiar with the normal appearances and special characteristics of each species before adjusting for Species rating, **Condition rating** or **Location rating** during a plant appraisal. (CTLA, 2000)

Cost and/or Actual Costs together, being careful not to add costs twice for the same task. Another option would be to determine Cure Costs and adding the Supplementary Cost. This option considers Years to Parity when the benefits cure cannot be made fully on the effective date as the curative plan is executed. This allows the appraiser to accomidate space limitations and use fewer plants to meet the anticipated benefits to be yielded at a future date.

In GPA9, compounding of costs was permitted in cost approach to value. This procedure is confusing because if the present value of the anticipated future benefits is a monetary equivalency, then the same money that is equivalent to anticipated benefits may be securely invested during the parity period for a similar return. If compounding were permitted, it would yield a future value, not present value as of the effective date. That is double dipping on the return of the money for the same benefits and the compounding procedure should be avoided.

Note: The subject trees of this example site were densely populated well past the point of superadequacy and were completely destroyed by the taking.

EXAMPLE

Tree Species Ratings

The species ratings were derived from the "Southeastern Species Rating Guide," July 2005. The species rating guide was developed and published by the Southern Chapter of the International Society of Arboriculture to assist PAs in determining the species ratings, basic values and costs basis in Alabama, Arkansas, Georgia, Louisiana, Mississippi, North Carolina, South Carolina and Tennessee. It is meant to be a supplement to the CTLA *Guide for Plant Appraisal, 9th Ed.* (Smiley 2005).

In this example, the Southeastern Species Rating Guide was used. An extensive survey of tree and plant management professionals was conducted and the data was compiled to calculate these ratings but not all regions use this same approach. Higher-rated species are considered to have more desirable characteristics than lower-rated species. Species rated lower than 50% are considered undesirable. The following tables show the species rating tabulations:

Species Depreciation in Cost to Cure

Tree Species #	Species	Common Name	Range	Rating %
1	Acer negundo	Boxelder	15-30	30%
2	Acer rubrum	Red Maple	80-95	90%
3	Acer saccharum	Sugar Maple	50-70	65%
4	Carya cordiformis	White Hickory	60-90	85%
5	Carya glabra	Pignut Hicory	70-85	80%
6	Carya ovata	Shagbark Hickory	60-80	70%
7	Celtis occidentalis	Common Hackberry	50-80	70%
8	Cornus florida	White dogwood	80-100	95%
9	Diospyros virginiana	Persimmon	50-80	75%
10	Fraxinus americana	White Ash	60-80	80%
11	Juglans nigra	Walnut	50-80	75%
12	Juniperous virginiana	60-80	60-80	75%
13	Morus sp.	Mulberry	30-60	55%
14	Nyssa sylvatica	Blackgum	75-95	90%
15	Prunus serrotina	Black Cherry	30-50	40%
16	Qurecus rubra	Red Oak	50-70	60%
17	Sassafras albidum	Sassafras	60-80	80%
Average			1215%	74.14%

EXAMPLE

Tree Condition Ratings

The condition ratings factors consist of the conditions of various anatomical tree structures that can have both structural and health importance. Broadly, these structures are the roots and buttress, trunk, **scaffold branches**, small branches, twigs, foliage and buds. Roots, trunk and scaffold branches are rated for both health and structure while leaves/buds and small branches/twigs are only rated for health. GPA9 condition rating was used in each broad category and rated from 1 to 4 for structure and (if applicable) 1 to 4 for health with potential maximum total of 32 points. I examined ten existing trees from the site for conditions and averaged their condition ratings. The total points from the ten sample trees was 185 points. The average tree condition rating for the site was 58%.

Note: While it is possible to reduce the condition for each broad category of pre-existing anatomical plant part to depreciation of individual benefits delivery, it was not necessary to perform that refinement in this assignment because the tree canopy was the primary benefits delivery anatomical structure and the other plant parts did not contribute much directly to the benefits delivery.

Placement Ratings

After careful consideration of the placement, species and site, I calculated a rating of 18%. The trees were situated where their aesthetic appearance could not be easily enjoyed. The fact that the subject trees were not well maintained, the lack of care given to site upkeep and the trashy appearance of tree debris on the ground also had a very negative impact on the aesthetic placement rating. There were piles of composted wood chips that could have been used to improve the appearance of walking trails and some of the nearby vegetation, but this was not done. There was very little in the way of maintenance that could have improved the delivery of the subject's functional and aesthetic benefits. The amount of tree canopy taken from the subject parcel was actually very small, being only 1,940 square feet of canopy. Although the site was suitable for greenway traffic and early successional wildlife refuge, these uses are limited by the installation of landowner fencing and the tree hazards that existed. The site also had severe planting restrictions posed by the presence of the pre-existing utility easements. The presence of the pre-existing 40' petroleum pipeline easements and transmission towers and lines with a 100' wide easement severely affected the species to site space for most of the focal trees. Had the trees been situated in a more favorable placement for the plants' mature size in the landscape, their usefulness might have been much better.

Tree Benefits to Landowners

Most of the trees that were cut offered very little in the form of ornamental aesthetic qualities. That being said, the eastern red cedars offered dark dense foliage and interesting trunk bark. The black cherries were a mix of good and bad. They offered interesting bark color and texture and some white color and sweet spring fragrance, but they also had bad problems with leaf spot disease, which disfigured the foliage. Because the trees were neglected, they suffered from black knot canker and other structural defects that took much of their ornamental value away. Black cherry trees harbor eastern tent caterpillars, whose presence are known to cause spontaneous foal abortions in horses and can be very detrimental to some types of agriculture. (Dirr, 1983; Gilman, 2004 et al.) The hackberries were also a mix of good and bad. They offered interesting bark color and textures, but hackberry nipple gall psyllids had infested the leaves, leaving them disfigured. Also, heavy infestations of Asian woolly aphids and their fecal products had caused black residue on the lower leaves and under the trees. Pruning neglect of these trees has caused canopy dieback and uncorrected growth defects, some of which have resulted in branch failures. The net result is that much of the ornamental character of these trees was diminished.

Boxelder bug susceptibility and canopy dieback are just two of the qualities that make boxelder trees undesirable. The wood is heavy and prone to breakage, putting anything that exists below (like cattle and other livestock) at risk. The tree has no redeeming qualities of landscape value.

The white ash trees are an excellent tree and have many fine qualities; however, the discovery of Emerald Ash Borer here in Tennessee has made the planting of any ash trees here untenable. Because of this formidable pest, it is recommended that ash trees not be planted and that has greatly diminished their landscape value here.

Sassafras is another valuable tree to any landscape; however, they are quite difficult to successfully transplant. The one specimen that was found was too small and there were not enough of these trees found at this site to contribute a significant ornamental value. Also, they are not widely available at nurseries.

The oak trees offer dominant and co-dominant tree canopy, hard mast food and habitat for advanced successional wildlife species. They also offer cooling shade for undergrowth species of plants and animals — they also suppress undesirable undergrowth. There were a few oaks on this site.

Hickory species offer food sources and habitat for advanced successional wildlife species. Walnut offers food for advanced successional wildlife; however, the presence of thousand cankers disease in Tennessee makes their sustained use untenable. Persimmon, red maples, sugar maples, mulberry and dogwoods offer food for birds and small animals.

The neglected and wild appearance, as well as other specific problems already discussed, significantly diminished the ornamental and

EXAMPLE

aesthetic contribution of the trees that were cut for the pipeline easement. Of all the potential use that these trees could have contributed to this site, only a tiny portion of these uses could be considered as practical function or aesthetic landscape use here.

The placement of trees is of significant importance to the overall opinion because placement is a determination of how well the trees can perform their functional and aesthetic purpose and use within the site. In this case, the focal trees' function and use was severely impeded by several factors.

Firstly, there were many tree trunks in a small space. This causes a phenomenon called tree trunk superadequacy — where the placement of too many trees (overpopulation) in a space can affect much lower amenity tree functions and uses than the well-planned spacing of professional landscape design that contains far fewer trees. The focal trees were severely overplanted, causing the vast majority of the trees to be superadequate. Because of this, the subject trees could never deliver the full function and use of individuals as one might expect in well-placed single specimen trees, like those in the nearby front yard.

Secondly, the trees that were taken nearby to the street lamp above the roadway were actually blocking light from the street lamp. Their location next to the lamp put those tree placements in conflict with the safety of those driving or walking along the road at night and created a liability. There were also utility lines and a flashing school sign connected to the same power pole. The branches and leaves of the trees were causing utility line clearance pruning activities to be routinely performed on those trees and they interfered with the utility facilities prior to the easement taking.

Thirdly, the presence of the TVA transmission lines and towers prior to the taking of the trees severely affected the appearance of the site and greatly diminished the aesthetic curb-appeal qualities of the trees that existed there. The transmission line easement also restricted greatly the types of flora that could be grown at the site prior to the taking. This also had a significantly negative affect on the opinion of tree value.

Plant Restoration and Establishment

Plant restoration and establishment depends on reasonable plans that use standard methods and procedures necessary to re-establish benefits of a vegetative area to near their pre-casualty condition. The appraiser should develop a system to employ one or more methods that, over time, will encourage re-establishment of plants based on the biological needs of the replacement species and their suitability of replacing amenity benefits.

An appraiser may estimate or obtain estimates from qualified contractors to establish a plant health care (PHC) program for plant restoration and establishment. A PHC program incorporates the implementation of integrated pest management (IPM) and other general plant care (planting, mulching, irrigation, pruning, fertilizing, etc.). IPM uses an inspection/treatment strategy that employs biological, cultural and chemical tactics. These tactics minimize insect and disease damage to the site and maximize opportunity for plant growth and overall health. After each inspection/treatment visit on the site, an IPM report is written so that the program will be documented for improved management.

Pruning to Improve Restoration of Plants

Pruning should be limited to removing damaged, dead, dying, diseased, broken, crossing, rubbing, or weakly attached branches because trees in damaged areas often expend energy on wound closure and defense from diseases. Such pruning may be done over two or more years.

Summary of Plant and Establishment Methods and Modified Cost of Cure

Estimated costs from restoration and establishment methods is added together to determine the Plant Restoration and Establishment. Total estimated cost in this Cost of Cure appraisal was performed consistent with the CTLA *Guide for Plant Appraisal, 9th Edition.* No individual trees were measured and valued independently nor were sample plots of trees that were cut. Nearby sample trees were examined and measured to determine their functional and aesthetic contribution to the site as a whole. All cut trees' functional and aesthetic contributions to the site as a whole element were considered. It is assumed that these trees contributed value to the site as a whole just prior to their taking.

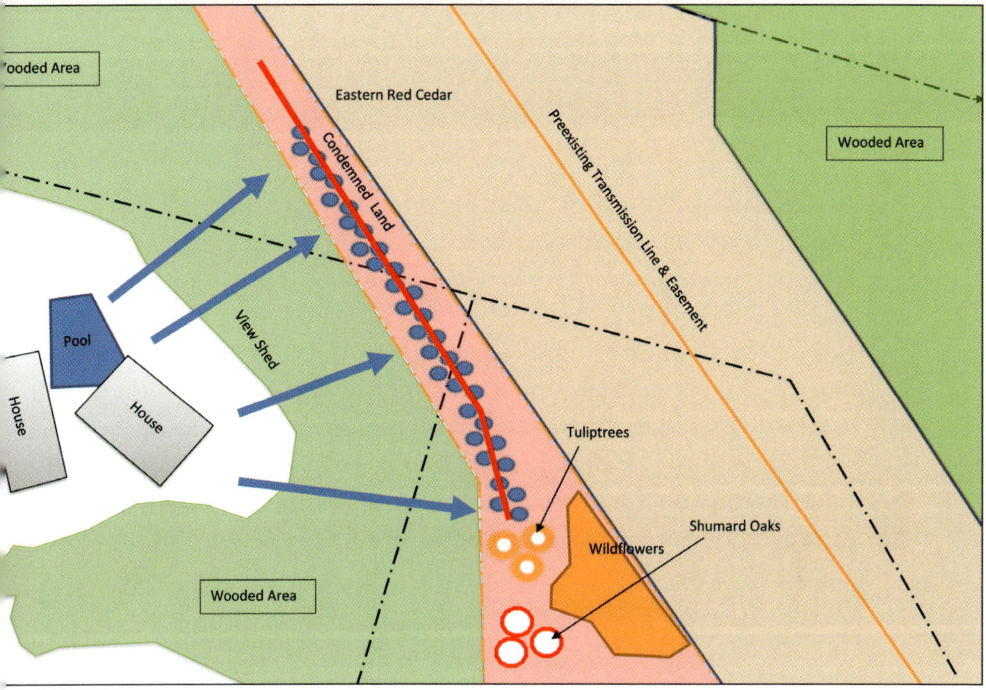

Site map shows recommended installation of curative trees.

EXAMPLE

Cure Design

Curative trees of this appraisal were selected based on their adaptability to the site and their ability to contribute both functionally and aesthetically. Specific suitable attributes were soil type, soil pH, soil nutrient levels, sun exposure, plant growth rate, USDA hardiness, ultimate height and spread at maturity, foliage persistence, canopy density, soil moisture content, seasonal interest, fall color, wildlife habitat, tree shape, root development, durability and structural strength. Curative trees were also selected for qualities that could improve their aesthetic and functional contribution to the site through better placement and spacing. The qualities that could be improved are landscape screening, ornamental aesthetics, transpirational cooling/livestock shelter, wildlife habitat, noise and odor attenuation and wind control. Curative tree sizes and conditions were determined by locating the largest commonly available, easily transportable and transplantable trees at local nurseries that were grown to ANSI Z60.1 Nursery Stock Standards.

EXAMPLE

Total CTLA Cost of Cure Appraised Value

The total CTLA Cost of Cure Appraised Value is $11,200.00.

Cost of Repair Calculation

If a tree defect is permanent, it is incurable and cannot be corrected through any means of repair treatment. If the defect can be cured through corrective repair treatment, it is considered curable and this distinction may become an important part of the cost appraisal problem. The PA must be familiar with the various defects and maladies that plants suffer and must be able to identify those visable defects and maladies that are curable and those that are incurable. When the malady or defect is curable, the appraiser may be able to form a reliable opinion on how much the curable condition will cost to remedy and to what extent the remedy will fix the lost delivery of benefits.

CHAPTER TWELVE

Income Approach

Another method to appraise the amenity value of subject trees is the Income Approach to value. This is typically the approach that is used when a landowner is seeking to derive income from the amenity trees that are growing on their land. A typical scenario to this approach would require an appraiser to calculate the amount of money that could be generated from the presence of the amenity trees growing on a piece of real estate; thus, the value is in the amount of income the trees can produce over time. An example might be the value of trees that provide shade for cattle that are to be sold at market or a type of wholesale nursery business that sells trees to landscape contractors, for example. There are also other forms of income, like the additional rents that can be derived from real estate because of tree benefits that are enjoyed by renters.

Income Tree Calculations

Cost approach value has been the courts' preference for amenity tree values in Tennessee since Jones v Johnson on June 4, 2003 and confirmed in Wood v Wolfenbarger, August 15, 2012. The Cost Approach methodology for diminution of value for trespass damage cases in Tennessee was first recounted in Jones v Johnson.

Operational financial performance is the chief indicator of income when income type of value is sought by the PA. Performance data can be obtained from business tax returns, customer sales receipts, expense receipts, income statements, profit and loss reports and asset/liability reports used in lending. Generally, profits are used to calculate income over time. Any amenity plant income valuation opinion will be calculated based on the cost of the initial investment and the amount of return on the investment as could be expected over a specific timeframe. The factor of earnings for the investment over time is called the rate of return.

While the GPA9 Income Approach procedure and methodology has sometimes been used for appraising income of trees as a part of real estate investments, it has limited application in appraising amenity tree tort damages to amenity trees at a wholesale/retail nursery business. While the GPA9 does allow for use of an income property's income stream and/or resale value to be capitalized into a present value, the basis for most Income Approach appraisal problems is a straightforward formula.

The GPA9 version is: **Annual** Income (profit) ÷ Rate of Return = Value.

The USPAP version is: Net Operating Income (NOI) ÷ Cap Rate = Value where NOI ÷ Sale Price = Cap Rate.

Market catalog pricing, actual sales transaction data, production cost data and/or profit and loss data indicate sales and income performance of products sold and all may be important in determining Gross Income. Operating Expenses and Cost of Goods Sold are generally subtracted from Gross Sales to calculate Gross Profit. While pricing catalogs and marketing materials may provide some indication of value for crops in the field, it is important to note that nurseries rarely sell all their crops. Likewise, nurseries often sell at a discount to catalog list prices for volume buyers. Also, crops in the field do not account for the all labor and materials needed to take a crop to market. Each nursery has its own business model and crop cycling. When crops become oversized, they can exceed the nursery model. In these situations, the existing crop is culled, and a new crop is planted. Since each income appraisal is specific to the business model of each nursery, careful examination of the model should be made to independently verify all data that is relevant to the appraisal problem.

The verification of transaction data is critical. The accumulation and analysis of customer sales transactions should include dates, quantities, sizes, species and sales prices of each plant/item sold and these transaction data should be considered as most reliable. Also, purchases for inputs/expenses should be likewise detailed for each vendor. Labor expense reports and overhead can also be scrutinized for verification.

The Cap Rate is used to determine the present value of future income. Although this method risks becoming somewhat circular without solid initial investment figures. Analysis of historical net income sales data, Costs of Goods Sold, overhead, expenses and labor can produce a credible income valuation. Obtaining detailed and accurate historical finance, sales, cost of goods sold and expense data is imperative when performing a standard income approach and methodology when an Income type of opinion to appraised value is needed. The appraiser must also make site visits to verify the quality, size and species of crops/landscaping that exist and to verify that the business operation has kept accurate records.

The advantage of the income approach is that it permits the appraiser to analyze the value of future income and performance, but it is considered less reliable for certain properties when there is a lack of relevant market/income data to support value conclusions. The Direct Capitalization methods are most often used for commercial properties with abundant sales, income, expense and other financial data. Direct Capitalization Method generally uses net Income/investment capitalization rate to calculate value. (Detty, Basic Appriaisal Proceedures, 2nd ed., 2007)

+ Effective Gross Income
- Cost of Goods Sold
- Labor
- Overhead
- Expenses
= Net Income

Cap Rate = Net Income/Value
Value x Cap Rate = Net Income
Net Income/Cap Rate = Value

A typical valuation for a profitable business should yield a 15-20% Cap Rate.

CHAPTER THIRTEEN

Sales Comparison Approach (Market)

When it comes to CREMV of amenity trees, it is an extremely difficult problem to solve because of the scant CREMV landscape improvement data to inform a sales comparison opinion. The most reliable means that may be employed to measure such a contribution is reconciled from both the unit cost of the installed nursery tree *and* the tree and landscaping benefits that are demanded by the pool of participants in the market place who prefer the relevant and specific property characteristics/benefits that mature trees and landscaping provide.

While this pool of participants may be smaller than the larger population in broader real estate markets, the fact that this pool of buyers exists and is reliable is born out of the fact that very large trees are bought, transported and transplanted at cost plus profit on a regular basis throughout the United States. Not everyone can afford to participate in that market pool, and care should be taken when placing large value on trees in locations where the actual transplantation of such trees is not realistically feasible. The market can supply a ready substitute at similar or less cost than is required for large tree transplantation, so long as the relevant characteristics sales data points can be reliably parsed from the market and is sufficiently abundant, local and current.

Important Real Estate Market Approach Appraisal Terms

While no single text can educate and prepare a PA to credibly and reliably perform real estate appraisals, there are some Market Approach terms that the PA should be familiar with:

Substitution

Substitution is a fundamental appraisal principle. It states that when several similar commodities, goods or services exist in a venue, people have a preference for the one with the lowest price and that the lowest price will always command the greatest demand and the widest distribution. Substitution is the primary principle upon which Cost and Sales Comparison (Market) approaches are based. Cost is typically dependent on production-new data points and Market is dependent on accurate and relevant sales data points. The question often arises as to which forces drive the most reliable economic model, Cost or Market? Without the introductions of new commodities, goods or services (Cost Approach), Market demand and pricing would spin wildly upward, out of control at inflationary rates. Without sufficient Market demand, no profitable Cost production would be possible. The reality is simple. Neither Cost Approach nor Market Approach is most reliable; they are simply different economic models that represent different economic perspectives of supply and demand in exchange. In real estate appraisal, there is a tendency toward Market Approach where comparative sales data is ready, relevant and reliable. Cost Approach is preferred where comparative sales data is scarce.

Anticipation

Anticipation is the human perception that value is created by an expectation of enjoying future benefits. It is this expectation that creates desire within the minds of all market participants and buyers of new goods, commodities and services. Sellers and producers count on this anticipation of enjoying benefits combined with scarcity to drive buyers to pay higher prices.

Fructus Naturales - Trees are Dirt?

Literally, the fruits of nature. When trees are sold at market as individually transported plants, they are personal property. Once they are planted in the ground, they become a permanent part of the real estate. Fruits, leaves and twigs that are attached are likewise part of the real estate, but when fruits, leaves and twigs fall, they become personal property, even if they create more maintenance then they are worth. When REAs look at trees they usually either see timber (Income Approach) or they see dirt (Vacant Property), and REAs do this regardless of the size, condition, species, placement of trees, landscaping, or the qualities any of the benefit producing characteristics that might be anticipated in use as landscape amenities by buyers and sellers in the real estate markets. In financial instruments like government-backed mortgages (about 99% of the uses of real estate appraisals), REAs are not required to consider trees and landscaping value in detail, and most REAs do not possess the requisite education, training, experience and skills to perform professional plant appraisals.

Fructus Industriales - Trees are Not Dirt?

Literally the fruits of industry, aka emblements or crops, which are commodities or the fruit of one's labor that are to be sold for money. Nursery crops are fructus industriales.

Highest and Best Use

In real estate analysis, it is the highest return of money of any property that should be made. Often the question of how a property should be used comes down to matter of money. A typical appraisal problem of highest and best use would be to answer a question of whether the current use of a real estate (the land and all of its improvements) would be worth more as vacant land and the costs to make it vacant. Another application to an HBU problem might be a monetary comparison as to whether or not there is a better return on investment income by renovating an existing land improvement or not. The question is answered by looking at the costs of the improvement and the difference in the income the renovated improvement will command in the market. If the CREMV of the renovated improvement will bring a higher market price or income than the investment costs of the renovations, the highest and best use is as a renovated improvement. Sometimes, if the land improvement has sufficient obsolescence, the highest and best use may include the cost of demolition so that the property can be sold on the market as vacant land.

Sales Comparison Approach

This is the process of distilling an indication of value of a subject property by comparing market sales data of several similar substitutes. This approach depends on obtaining reliable data that contains similar, relevant characteristic sales data points that are comparable to the subject. The comparable sales figure data is adjusted based on the qualitative and quantitative benefits that the market anticipates from the substitutes. Value opinion in the Sales Comparison Approach (Market Approach) is based on parity sales comparisons of the subject.

It is nearly impossible to do this type of comparison with amenity landscaping and trees because the relevant characteristic comparative sales data for amenity trees and landscaping does not exist in any of the relevant real estate sales market data sets. There is a little research that suggests (generally) that trees may have some sort of contribution to the value of real estate, but these research papers have very little to do with CREMV of landscape trees and are very unreliable for the following reasons:

CREMV calculations require the identifying following relevant characteristics:

- Size of trees and landscape elements
- Conditions of trees and landscape elements
- Species of trees and landscape elements
- Placement of trees and landscape elements
- Site conditions to species

CREMV calculations require the following types of comparative sales data:

- Large pools of data must be obtained (perhaps five-to-ten properties).
- Data must be current to the effective date of the appraisal. Sales that are too old will not be considered relevant. Usually, within six months.
- The data must be relevant. With trees, that means that the comparative data must contain the size, species, condition, location and other landscape characteristics parsed in the sales transaction for comparison.
- Only local property sales data that is similar to the subject property may be used. That means you must use parcels with similar improvements (such as trees) that are similar to the subject as well as buildings and other structures.

If these criteria cannot be met because of SOW limitations or because of the scarcity of comparative sales data, then Cost Approach or Income Approach must be used instead. Keep in mind that governmental zoning restrictions, like single family residential (R1), may limit such amenity plant appraisals to cost since an R1 resident owner, may not be legally permitted to operate a going concern. If the subject is an income property it may be possible to calculate a loss in rents that is attributable to amenity landscaping and trees. As with Market Approach, similar income properties and the landscape characteristics would need to be distilled from the income data for an apples-to-apples comparison analysis.

Paired Data Analysis

Paired data analysis is a quantitative technique used to identify and account for adjustments to the sale price or rents due to a comparable property's physical characteristics. To apply this technique, sales or rental data on nearly identical properties is analyzed to isolate and estimate a single characteristic's effect on the value of the whole. Often referred to as paired sales analysis.

For the correct procedure of applying paired data analysis, the market appraiser must be able to identify the relevant characteristics of the subject, find current, locally suitable substitutes with the same or very similar characteristics and calculate the CREMV of each of those characteristics using shared data point repository systems of accumulated data that has been recorded by other market appraisers sharing the same market data.

The difficulty in using this method in professional plant appraisal is that the relevant data point characteristics of tree size, species, placement, condition, benefits and delivery are not recorded or shared among the real estate appraisal community.

Land Improvement

Improvements are buildings, structures or some otherwise permanently developed modifications to the land involving expenditures of labor and capital that are intended to enhance the value or utility of the property. Improvements can be any elements of value that require human agency, proximity or planning that are located on or attached to the land for enhanced use.

Trees that are planned and planted for amenity use, such as landscape amenities, are improvements. Also, trees that are cultivated, managed and maintained in use as landscape amenities are also considered improvements, even if their origin (natural or otherwise) is not known. It is the anticipated use of their functional and aesthetic amenity benefits that makes trees and shrubs valuable as improvements to the land.

Quantitative Adjustment

In the Sales Comparison Approach, the process of making numerical adjustments to the sale price of comparable properties, including data analysis techniques (paired data analysis, grouped data analysis and secondary data analysis) statistical analysis, graphic analysis, trend analysis, cost analysis (cost-to-cure, depreciated cost) and capitalization of rent differences usually precedes qualitative adjustments.

Quantitative Techniques

Quantitative techniques are those used in the Comparative Sales Approach to derive quantitative adjustments to sales prices of comparable properties.

Also used in other valuation approaches and techniques, such as graphic analysis, grouped data analysis, paired data analysis, statistical analysis, trend analysis and cost analysis.

Quantitative Variable

A variable that can be measured numerically. Examples in Sales Comparison Approach in real estate appraisal include measurable items, such as living space, number of bathrooms, number of bedrooms and size of the parcel. In the Cost Approach of plant appraisal, it is the measurements of trunk area, canopy volume or canopy area; or other quantitative or functional benefits.

Qualitative Analysis

Qualitative analysis is the process of accounting for the differences between subject property and the corresponding characteristics of comparable, replacement or curative properties that are not quantified. Qualitative analysis may be combined with quantitative analysis to allow qualitative measurements to take on quantitative character. Functional benefits of amenity trees and shrubs tend to be quantitative in nature while the aesthetic benefits and characteristics are more difficult to measure. When quantitative analysis is accompanied by qualitative analysis, the combined analysis takes on quantitative character. Appraised values are more credible when form (qualitative attributes) follows function (quantitative attributes).

CHAPTER FOURTEEN

Reporting

THE FIRST ASCA BOOK PUBLICATION, *GUIDE TO REPORT Writing for Consulting Arborists,* was an excellent reference that established the basic structure of professional plant appraisal reports back in 1995. In 2000, GPA9 included an entire section that outlined the qualifications of PAs and included an outline of the various written report formats. In 2004, ASCA came out with a refinement in guidance to report writing with *A Consultant's Guide to Writing Effective Reports*, which offers a wealth of information on proper structure when writing form, letter and booklet report formats and I cannot add any report writing refinements to these fine publications at this time. One area that ASCA and CTLA do not address is that of oral reporting. (ASCA, 2004) (Council of Tree and Landscape Appraisers, 2000) (ASCA, 1995)

Depending on how the report will be used, the reporting options are selected based on their appropriateness to their use. Clients who simply need a quick number to permit an informed decision may only need an oral report while cases that involve complex issues and careful consideration of the appraisal questions may require a booklet report. Between these report formats there are also forms, which require little preparation, or letters, which are useful in preliminary findings, where the scope of work tends to be more limited.

Oral Reports

Oral reports can be useful for clients who will use the conclusions of your report for straightforward decision making. They are brief and concise. While the report itself does not leave a paper trail, the work that goes into preparing the oral report most certainly does. All of the work that went into preparing your opinion of appraised value must be kept in the work file for the assignment. This includes records of phone conversations, personal notes, observations, any photos you took or looked at and a list of references you consulted. The file may include copies of survey records, warranty deeds, deposition transcripts, interrogatories, other appraisals, expert reports, billing information and any other thing that went in to preparing your opinion and it must include a record of the date and time that you transmitted the report to your client.

Form Reports

The GPA9 (2000) forms are very useful for collecting much of the relevant quantitative field data for the appraisal and they are very handy for record keeping purposes. CTLA forms are not suitable for some of the refinement found in this book. I have crafted field data collection template forms to assist you in identifying the relevant characteristics on site. There is a template for calculating unit cost, depreciation and a spreadsheet that contains many of the calculations you will need to perform; it is available at http://www.ProAPAH.com/forms, click on the form you need and enter the code: ProForms.

Letter Format Reports

Components:

Summary
Assignment
Problem ID
Scope of Work
Background
Observations
Testing and Analysis
Discussion
Conclusion
Recommendation (optional)

The summary of a letter report is a critical component of the report. It permits the reader to quickly ascertain the report contents, quickly recall report content and retain a brief file reference to the completed work. At a minimum, the summary should have the important opinions and conclusions that are developed because of an investigation. (ASCA, 1995)

GPA9 guidance requires that Observation, Analysis or Testing, Appraisal Procedures and Discussion of how the appraiser's opinions were formed be included in the letter report. The letter PAL report must also include a well-defined assignment that includes details of the subject plants being appraised, details of the subject property, details of the purpose and use of the appraisal and a definition of value that is clear to the appraisal users and that aligns with the purpose of the appraisal. USPAP guidelines also suggest that the appraisal problem be properly framed by identifying who the client is, who the intended users are, the type of value being sought, the effective date of the opinion of value, the relevant characteristics of the items being appraised and any assignment conditions, such as any extraordinary assignment assumptions or any hypothetical conditions.

Booklet Format Reports

Components:

1. Cover Letter
2. Title Page
3. Table of Contents
4. Summary
5. Introduction
6. Appraisal Assignment ID
    a. Client
    b. Intended Use
    c. Type and Definition of Value Sought (Purpose)
    d. Effective Date
    e. Subject Property Description
    f. Subject Plants Description
    g. Relevant Characteristics
    h. Assignment Conditions
7. Scope of Work Limits
8. Background
9. Observations
    a. Plant Size
    b. Plant Species

   c. Plant Conditions
      i. Leaves, Buds and Flowers
      ii. Limbs/Branches
      iii. Scaffold Branches
      iv. Trunk
      v. Buttress/Roots
   d. Age?
   e. Other Characteristics
   f. ID Functional Benefits
   g. ID Aesthetic Benefits
   h. ID Obsolescence
   i. Plant Placement
   j. Species/Site Suitability
   k. Species/Placement Suitability
   l. Other Obsolescence

10. Methods
11. Testing and Analysis
   a. Lab Tests and Analysis
   b. Diagnostic Procedures
   c. Appraisal Procedures
   b. Subject Data Analysis
12. Discussion
   a. Explanation of methodology and reasoning for opinion of value
   b. Each discussion topic may contain an opinion of that topic
13. Conclusions
14. Certification
15. Notarization/Affidavit (if required)
16. Recommendations
17. Supporting Information
18. Appraisers Credentials
19. Supporting Documentation
   a. Tables
   b. Photos
   c. Maps Plans
   d. Drawings and Figures
   e. Glossary
   f. Bibliography
   g. Other Supporting Documents

CHAPTER FIFTEEN

Some Concluding Thoughts on Amenity Plant Appraisal

It has been said in various ways throughout this book — and many times over the years by other professional amenity plant appraisers — that amenity plant and landscape appraisal is not simple, and it is not easy. Valuation problems can seem, on their surface, simple and straightforward. In reality, they can be very complex and nuanced. They also range widely in scope from opinions that are based on minimal data to assignments that require large amounts of data collection and rigorous analysis.

What I have attempted to do, within the confines of these few pages, is to create a desktop reference that permits professional amenity plant appraisers to:

- Identify the appraisal problems they are called upon to solve,
- Identify the various types and definitions of value that amenity plant appraisers may be called upon to solve,
- Develop scopes of work plans that will aid them in finding credible results,
- Identify the relevant subject characteristics upon which amenity plant worth is based,
- Identify the anticipated amenity benefits upon which an amenity plant's worth hinges,
- Correctly analyze and process the relevant data facts for the various approaches and methodologies that amenity plant appraisers must use to solve PAL problems, and
- Correctly and appropriately report their appraisal results to their clients.

I have also included a glossary of terms and an index as quick reference aids to assist the appraiser in understanding the terminology, the systematic process and the overall practice of PAL.

This reference includes enough detail to point plant appraisers in the direction of researching the critical subject matter that may be relevant to their assignments, but it is no substitute for the plant appraiser's own need to have a thorough and knowledgeable understanding of the various assignment elements they take on and opine about. Only a small portion of this book will be useful for any given individual assignment, but as the plant appraiser expands his or her areas of expertise and competence by taking on more and varied types of plant appraisal work, this book will become an indispensable, go-to resource and a reference for guidance in the various appraisal tasks that plant appraisers are assigned.

Over the years, I have accumulated just enough competence that I now feel confident to write authoritatively about this subject matter. I have read hundreds of books, attended hundreds of hours of training sessions, looked up thousands of references and consulted with hundreds of varied subject matter experts. It would behoove any plant appraiser at most any level of competence to do the same for subjects that are unfamiliar to them. It is a journey that both challenges the professional and rewards. It is a journey that is unquestioningly well worth the taking. It is a journey that will last a lifetime.

GLOSSARY

Acronyms

ACFA: Association of Consulting Foresters of America
ALSO: Amenity Landscape Shade and Ornamental (Trees)
ANLA: American Nursery and Landscape Association
ANSI: American National Standards Institute
ANSI Z60.1: In the United States, industry-developed national standards for nursery stock.
ANSI A300: In the United States, industry-developed national consensus standards of practice for tree care.
ASCA: American Society of Consulting Arborists
ASLA: American Society of Landscape Architects
BCMA: Board Certified Master Arborist
CTLA: Council of Tree and Landscape Appraisers
DBH: Diameter at Breast Height
GPA9: *Guide for Plant Appraisal, 9th Edition*
IPM: Integrated Pest Management
ISA: International Society of Arboriculture
ISO: International Standards Organization
NALP: National Association of Landscape Professionals
NESC: National Electric Safety Code
NDVI: Normalized Difference Vegetation Index
PA: Professional Amenity Plant Appraiser
PAL: Professional Amenity Plant Appraisal
PHC: Plant Health Care
ProAPAH: *Professional Amenity Plant Appraisal Handbook*
RA or REA: Real Estate Appraiser
REAL: Real Estate Appraisal
RCA: Registered Consulting Arborist
ROW: Right-of-Way
TCIA: Tree Care Industry Association
TRAQ: Tree Risk Assessment Qualification
USDA: United States Department of Agriculture
USPAP: Uniform Standards of Professional Appraisal Practice

Definitions

Absorb: To take up.

Acid: Having a pH of less than 7.0 (contrast with alkaline).

Adaptable: Genetic ability of plants and other living organisms to adjust or acclimate to different environments.

Aerobic: Having no restriction in the supply of oxygen.

Aesthetic: Pleasing to the senses, visually or otherwise. Evoking a good feeling.

Aesthetic Benefits: The benefits of landscape trees and plants, characterized by their ability to be measured qualitatively in their artistic use in landscape architectural design. Evaluation of aesthetic benefits requires qualified judgments and reasoning and is more subjective to the appraiser's training, skill, experience and education in landscaping than are functional benefits; therefore, aesthetic benefits are considered subordinate to functional benefits.

Aggregate: A material or structure formed from a loosely compacted mass of fragments or particle; in soil it is the larger than sand components mostly comprised of stone and small rocks; in concrete it is the rocky material that is larger than sand.

Algae: A simple nonflowering plant of a large group that includes the seaweeds and many single-celled forms. Algae contain chlorophyll but lack true stems, roots, leaves and vascular tissue.

Alkaline: Having a solution pH greater than 7.0 (contrast with acidic).

Amenity: 1) A desirable and/or useful feature or facility of a building, a place, or a landscape; 2) a feature that increases attractiveness or value, especially of a piece of property.

Amenity Plant: Any desirable live plant in functional and aesthetic use by people or wildlife, particularly in improvements landscaping or as habitat for wildlife.

American National Standards Institute: A private non-profit organization that oversees the development of voluntary consensus standards for products, services, processes, systems, personnel and units of measure in the United States.

Annual: Anything that recurs each year.

Appraisal: 1) The process of placing a monetary value on a property; 2) in professional amenity plant appraisal specialty, the process of placing a monetary value on amenity trees, plants, or other landscaping, including ancillary landscape features of an entire property; 3) a report stating an opinion of Appraised Value.

Appraised Value: See assignment results.

Arboriculture: Practice and study of the care of trees and other woody plants in the landscape.

Arborist: Professional who possesses the technical competence gained through experience and related training to provide for or supervise the management of trees and other woody plants in residential, commercial and public landscapes.

Arm's Length: In real estate transactions, it is the principle that states all parties in a real estate deal are acting in their own self-interests and are not compelled to engage in the transaction from the other parties. For example: property sales between family members are not arm's length because the buyer and the seller may not be acting with disinterest of the other party.

Assignment Results: 1) An appraiser's opinion and conclusions that are developed for an assignment. In professional amenity plant appraisal, it includes a monetary value; 2) a review opinion as to the relevance, adequacy, or reasonableness of an opinion developed by another appraiser's assignment; 3) a recommendation opinion developed in an appraisal consulting assignment.

Bacteria: Single-celled organisms having a cell wall but no organized nucleus.

Bark: Protective outer covering of branches and stems that arises from the cork **cambium**.

Best Management Practices: Best-available, industry-recognized courses of action, in consideration of the benefits and limitations, based on scientific research and current knowledge.

Branch: Stem arising from a larger stem. A subdominant stem.

Bulk Density: Dry mass of soil per unit of volume, often used as a measure of compaction.

Buttress: Base of the tree where it enters the ground. Normally forms a flare where roots and trunk come together.

Caliper: Thickness or diameter of the trunk of a tree taken at a standard height (usually 6–10 inches above the ground) in ANSI Z60.1 nursery stock standards.

Canker: Localized diseased area on stems, roots and branches. Often sunken and discolored.

Canopy: Collective branches and foliage of a tree or group of trees' crowns. Aggregate or collective tree crowns.

Carbohydrate: Compound combining carbon and water in plants as a result of photosynthesis. Sugars, starches and cellulose.

Carbon Dioxide: A colorless gas, soluble in water, used in green plants to make carbohydrates. One of the important greenhouse gasses. While the effect of carbon dioxide sequestration is of debatable scientific significance in global climate change, it is certainly of great political interest worldwide. Carbon taxation and credits are a real and tangible governmental force in which trees may play a role.

Carbon Sequestration: Capturing and long-term storage of carbon. Most often used in reference to the capturing and retention of atmospheric carbon dioxide through biological, chemical, or physical processes. Trees sequester carbon through photosynthesis.

Cellulose: Complex carbohydrate found in the cell walls of most plants, algae and certain fungi. A major component of wood fibers.

Chronic: Disorder or disease occurring over a long period of time.

Clay: 1) Soil particles with a typical grain size of less than 0.004mm; 2) a soil predominantly composed of such particles, typically considered less fertile than most other soils.

Clearance: Amount of open space between a tree or tree part and another object, the ground, a pedestrian, or vehicle traffic on the ground. Often used in reference to the distance between trees and utility lines or trees and buildings.

Condition Rating: In GPA9, one of three criteria used to calculate obsolescence in the cost approach to amenity tree appraisals. Standard Condition Ratings are comprised total of 62 individual condition elements that weigh both the structural integrity and for the health conditions of a tree's roots, trunk, scaffold branch, small branches, twigs and leaves. Each element is carefully weighed on a scale from one to four on five areas for health and three elements for structure. A maximum possible total of 32 points is given for a tree with no defects or a minimum of eight points for a tree with severe defects. The total points given is divided by 32 and multiplied by 100 to arrive at Condition Rating %. Some professional discretion is allowed in judging each individual condition element within the 32-point scale. For example, dead trees are usually given a Condition Rating of 0% as amenities even though the wood fiber could be useful for wood product production. Also see Location Rating and Species Rating.

Concrete: Freshly poured concrete is a thick fluid mixture of aggregate (typically limestone), sand and Portland cement. It starts out as a plastic mass that can be molded into virtually any shape, but as the material hardens, it changes chemically and there is a reduction in volume or what is more commonly known as shrinkage.

Consulting Arborist: Arboricultural or other expert who, through training, knowledge and experience, investigates tree-related matters, including but not limited to land assessments, tree canopy assessments, plant appraisals, tree hazard evaluations, tree risk assessments, or analytical testing services. They are frequently involved in forensic and other investigations and are skilled at reporting. Many also provide expert witness services.

Cost to Cure: Method used to appraise the monetary value of tree and landscape losses based on the treatment needed to return the benefits produced by a property to a reasonable approximation of its original condition when damage to ancillary items and/or changes in site topography have occurred or where trunk super adequacy exists. Also used to cure the remainder property in condemnation cases where the remainder property is diminished by the taking activities.

Cost of Repair: In tree damage cases, method used to appraise the monetary value of tree or plant losses by calculating the cost to repair or restore damaged tree parts to near the pre-damaged quality, condition and size. Essentially, it is the amount of money it costs to produce the functional and aesthetic benefits of amenity plants that are lost due to damage.

Council of Tree and Landscape Appraisers: Group of representatives of several tree care and landscape associations that works to author the *Guide for Plant Appraisal*. As of the writing of this book in 2017, the current edition is the 9th iteration.

Credibility: The state of being worthy of belief.

Cultivar: A nursery cultivated variety of plant. Cannot be reproduced without the aid of human assistance. Propagated through cloned cuttings or other non-sexual means.

Danger Tree: Any tree that, on failure, is capable of interfering with the safe, reliable transmission or distribution of electricity. If such trees exist near power lines, the responsible utility is obliged to mitigate them.

Decay: 1) An area of wood that is undergoing decomposition; 2) a process of degradation whereby wood is dissolved by fungi and other microorganisms.

Deciduous: Tree or other plant with leaves that undergo metamorphosis and that sheds all of their leaves before producing new leaves annually. Controlled genetically and influenced by climate, particularly cold temperatures and shorter day lengths.

Decline: Gradually diminishing health or condition of a tree.

Defect: An imperfection, weakness, or lack of something necessary. In trees, defects are injuries, growth patterns, decay, or other conditions that reduce the tree's structural strength.

Deficiency: 1) Pertaining to plant nutrition, lack or insufficient quantity of a required element; 2) pertaining to the plant's ability to deliver benefits. See obsolescence.

Dendrochronological: Pertaining to the study of age of wood, particularly growth rings. Since trees produce new growth rings each year, the study of growth rings provides a historically accurate way to measure the age of wood and the rate at which trees have grown over time. Growth patterns may indicate environmental changes, tree injury events and even tree death dates.

Design Criteria: Aspects of the landscape or site and the required functions to be served by the plant that must be considered in plant selection.

Dieback: Condition in which the progressive death of small twigs, twigs, limbs and branches in the tree crown die from the tips toward the trunk. Can be caused by many factors. (See inner canopy dieback)

Canopy Area: Area within the drip line.

Drip Line: Imaginary line that vertically traces the circumference of a trees canopy on the ground. Commonly traced at the tree canopy edge when seen from aerial photographs.

Drilling Resistance Technology: An invasive technique used to detect the relative strength of wood. Useful in detecting decay and growth rate of wood in live trees or wood products.

Drought: Period of unusually low precipitation.

Duty of Care: The legal obligation that requires an individual to apply reasonable actions when performing tasks that may potentially harm another.

Easement: A legal contract that gives the right to use another's land for a stated purpose. Includes Right-of-Ways.

Ecology: The study of the relationships between organisms and other living and nonliving elements of their environment.

Ecosystem: Complex system of living organisms and their abiotic environments.

Ecosystem Services: The benefits that people obtain from ecosystems.

Erosion: The wearing away of the land by the movement of water, wind, or ice.

Estate: 1) A right or interest in a property. Defines an owner's degree, quality, nature and extent of interest in a real property. There are many different types of estates, including freehold (fee simple, determinable fee and life estate) and leasehold. To be an estate in land, an interest must allow possession (either now or in the future) and be differentiated primarily by its duration. 2) The net worth of an entity at a point in time. Possessions left to heirs upon death are often referred to as the estate.

Essential Nutrients: Seventeen minerals essential to the growth and development of trees. These minerals are essential because plants cannot complete their life cycle without them.

Establish: To grow or cause a plant to grow successfully in a new place or refers to the care of trees in order to assure success after transplanting.

Evergreen: Tree or other plant that does not shed all its foliage annually and retains chlorophyll in the leaves (contrast with deciduous).

Exotic Plants: Non-native plant species. Some (a few) exotic plants are invasive and have resulted in both economic, environmental and ecological damage of high magnitude.

Failure: Uprooting or mechanical breakage of a tree, its parts and/or associated soil.

Failure Potential: In tree risk assessment (ANSI A300 Part 9), the professional assessment of the likelihood (probability) for a tree or tree part to fail within a defined timeframe.

Failure Rate: The relative rate that tree species with defects fail, usually expressed as low, medium, or high.

Fee Simple: The highest possible unencumbered ownership interest that can be held in real property, subject only to the limitations imposed by the governmental powers of taxation, eminent domain, police power and escheat.

Flower: Organ of sexual reproduction in angiosperms. In landscape design, certain desirable plant species, cultivars and varieties are selected for their impressive display of colorful and showy flowers.

Foliage: Leaves of a plant. In landscape architectural design, it is often the single most important and redundant attribute of plants and is the plant part that offers the greatest number of benefits. It is the plant anatomical structure that is responsible for texture, glossiness and certain dynamic seasonal interest characteristics or non-dynamic characteristics and gives plants their distinctiveness due to size and shape. Leaves are the most common means of identifying the genus and species of plants. Leaves are also the most important anatomical structure to produce photosynthate and to affect plant health.

Forensic: Pertaining to legal proceedings, often in context to evidence or testimony.

Functional Benefits: In landscaping, the benefits of landscape trees and plants, characterized by their ability to be measured quantitatively or their constructive use that may be replaced conventionally. The measurable services that trees provide.

Functional Goals: In landscape architectural design, the cumulative set of goals pertaining to the future needs, practical uses and intended purposes of each design site.

Green Infrastructure: Living plants and natural materials within developed areas that offer benefits and services like storm water management, erosion control, temperature mitigation, wind mitigation, light mitigation, carbon sequestration, traffic control and many others.

Ground: The earth's surface and everything beneath it. Dirt.

Ground Cover: Low-growing plants that require minimal maintenance, used in landscaping instead of turf or mulch.

Groundwater: Water that is naturally stored long-term in the ground as the result of precipitation, absorption, peculation and, eventually, infiltration. Precipitation above field capacity results in runoff. Synonym: aquifer.

Growth Rate: Speed at which something grows.

Habit: Characteristic form or manner of growth.

Habitat: An environment suitable for sustaining a population of a given organism.

Hardiness: Genetically determined ability of a plant to survive at low temperatures.

Hardscape: The inertly constructed elements of a landscape design, such as arbors, pergolas, decks, steps, railings, walls, pathways, benches, statuary and decorative elements made of conventional construction materials or art mediums. Not trees, plants and other living landscape elements.

Hazard: A tree or tree part identified as a likely source of harm.

Hazardous Condition: Situation that is likely to lead to a loss, personal injury, or property damage.

Hemicellulose: Substances that occur as constituents of plant cell walls and are polysaccharides of simpler molecular configuration than cellulose.

Hydrology: The branch of science concerned with water movement in relation to land and to the atmosphere.

Imminent Danger: An American legal concept describing "certain danger, immediate and impending; menacingly close at hand and threatening." In naval terms, collision imminent is a warning of the 100% certain collision of two ships or the ship and land that will occur within moments, which coincides with an alarm and a verbal warning to brace for impact. Also called "imminent danger."

Impervious: Surface that does not allow for percolation, infiltration, or absorption by water or other liquids. A characteristic of ground surfaces that contribute to runoff and prohibits water from entering the aquifer.

Infiltration: The downward movement of water into the soil.

Infiltration Rate: Speed at which water penetrates the soil.

Inflorescence: Cluster of flowers.

Inner Canopy Dieback: Natural and normal tree condition in which small twigs, twigs, small limbs and small branches die near to the trunk as a result of being shaded by larger and more vigorous upper canopy limbs, branches and foliage.

Integrated Pest Management: Method of controlling pests by combining cultural, biological and chemical management practices and strategies.

ISA Board Certified Master Arborist®: An arborist who has achieved the highest technical credential offered by International Society of Arboriculture and who maintains continuing education and who agrees to adhere to the ISA's Board Certified Master Arborist® Code of Ethics. ISA Board Certified Master Arborist is a registered trademark of the International Society of Arboriculture.

Landscape: The outdoor portion of a real property containing amenity tree, plant and other improvements that is used by people for landscaping purposes.

Landscape Architectural Design: Landscape architecture is the use of trees, plants and other ancillary elements to design outdoor areas that produce functional, environmental, social-behavioral, or other aesthetic benefits that have worth above vacant land. The design of such improvements is the systematic application of landscape architectural principals.

Landscape Screen: In landscape architecture, an aesthetic and functional use of landscape trees or large shrubs to partition an area or create an attractive visual barrier to an undesirable view. Screens can completely block a view or can diminish the visual impact of an undesirable feature through the use of more attractive and eye-catching plant features.

Leaf: Primary photosynthetic organ of a plant that is connected to a stem by a petiole. Primary source of plant health and delivery of functional and aesthetic amenity plant benefits.

Lignin: Organic compound that impregnates certain cell walls to thicken and strengthen the cell and to inhibit many forms of decay, fungi and other pests. Essentially it is the glue-like substance that holds cellulose fibers together in woody tissues.

Limb: 1) Large structure that supports a tree's canopy; 2) secondary order of limb structure, smaller and subordinate to scaffold limbs but superior to and larger than small branches and twigs.

Limiting Factor: An environmental characteristic or element that, when absent or in low measure, does not bound the growth of plants.

Liner: A nursery trade term of young, immature trees, shrubs, or smaller plants held for one, two, or three cycles as they mature to a commercially saleable size. A standard liner container is 9 cm in diameter (3.5").

Linkages: 1) A time and distance relationship between land use and support services and facilities as a benefit or convenience; 2) transportation time and costs for moving people to and from a site; 3) the harmonizing or disharmonizing relationship of uses among various properties in a group.

Litter: Decomposing but recognizable leaves and other debris forming a layer on top of the soil, especially in forests. Duff.

Loam: Soil texture classification consisting of somewhat less clay and more or less equal parts sand and silt. Considered ideal texture for plant growth.

Location Rating: In GPA9, one of three criteria used to calculate obsolescence in the cost approach to amenity tree appraisals. Standard Location Ratings consist of evenly weighted sub-factors of site, contribution and placement of trees in the landscape. Site is determined by looking at economic, functional and aesthetic aspects of properties surrounding the subject and the general appearance and conditions of the subject property in comparison. Contribution is concerned with the eleven aesthetic factors and fourteen functional factors affecting contribution. Knowledge of plant functions and uses and practical knowledge about the plant's ability to perform those functions and uses in a given situation is important in contribution. Some professional expertise is required to determine the contribution rating. Placement is concerned with how well the tree is placed in the landscape to provide its functional and aesthetic contributions from 10 to 100%. Each location sub-factor is expressed as a percent and they are averaged. Also see Condition Rating and Species Rating for other forms of cost depreciation.

Macronutrient: Essential plant element that is required in comparatively large quantities (contrast with micronutrient).

Micronutrient: Essential plant element that is required in comparatively small quantities (contrast with macronutrient).

Mineral: Naturally occurring inorganic solid that has chemical composition, characteristics and physical properties and are the primary source of soluble plant nutrients as they undergo changes due to biological activity and weathering.

Mitigation: 1) The method of reducing risk; 2) the act or planned activity to solve a non-appraisal related problem.

Moss: A small flowerless green plant that lacks true roots, growing in low carpets or rounded cushions in damp habitats and reproducing by means of spores released from stalked capsules.

Mutual Property Boundary: A real property boundary that adjoins two or more properties from which a commonly owned tree might originate at the base.

Mycorrhizae: Symbiotic associations between certain fungi and the roots of plants.

National Electric Safety Code: The standards adopted by most states and public utilities adapted to safeguarding persons during the installation, operation, repair, or maintenance of electrical supply and communication lines and associated facilities.

Nuisance: 1) A legal term meaning that an imminent threat of harm to people or property exists because of a condition; 2) a legal term meaning that a neighboring condition prevents the full legally permissible and reasonable use of one's property; 3) something that is problematic or a vexation.

Normalized Difference Vegetation Index: Used with satellite or drone cameras or sensors in agriculture, it measures the relative light frequency reflected from plant leaves as an indicator of plant health. The more detected plant reflected light in the corresponding frequency reflected by chlorophyll (mostly green bands) indicates greater plant health.

Obsolescence: 1) A deduction in a value opinion for any reason; 2) one cause of depreciation; 3) an impairment of desirability and usefulness due to more recent development of newer product innovations in design or manufacture or external factors that make an appraisal subject less desirable and less valuable in use. In the appraisal of plants, it is the loss in value due to physical deterioration of plant parts, loss in value because of poor design or landscape placement of the plant species, or loss in value due to poor species adaptability to site conditions.

Organic: Carbon containing substance; normally humic acids and other substances from decaying plant and animal matter.

Organic Matter: Dead remains of organisms in the process of decay by actions from live organisms like composted mulches derived from wood products. The bioactive, organic components of soil.

Penetrometer: A device for assessing soil resistance relative to soil moisture.

Permeability: A measure of the ease with which fluids (like water) can move through a porous soil.

Pest: Any organism that is undesirable.

Pesticide: Any chemical used to control or kill unwanted plants, animals, or fungi.

pH: A figure expressing the acidity or alkalinity of a solution on a logarithmic scale on which 7 is neutral, lower values are more acid and higher values more alkaline. The pH is equal to -log10c, where c is the hydrogen ion concentration in moles per liter.

Photosynthate: The products of photosynthesis and all subsequent biochemical reactions. The beginning of the biosynthetic pathway in plants.

Photosynthesis: The process in green plants (and algae and some bacteria) by which light energy from the sun is used to form carbohydrates (chemical energy) from water in the soil and carbon dioxide in the air. The process gives off oxygen.

Physiology: Study of plant form and function. It breaks plants down and studies specific organs and their functions or processes.

Pine: Common name given to gymnosperms (conifers) of the Pinacea family and Pinus genus.

Plant Selection: A function of landscape architectural design, it is the systematic process of analyzing the landscape design space, identifying the characteristics of the planting site and identifying the species, variety, or cultivar of plant that is best suited to the intended purpose of the design.

Plant Health Care: Comprehensive maintenance program designed to manage the health, structure and appearance of plants in their delivery of landscape amenity benefits.

Pore Space: Air- or water-filled spaces between solid soil particles.

Porosity: A measure of how much open space there is in soils. Large spaces containing gasses are called macropores and spaces capable of containing liquids are called micropores. High porosity indicates high permeability and low porosity indicates high bulk density and compaction.

Pruning: Removing branches (or occasionally roots) from a tree or other plant, using approved practices, to achieve a specified objective.

Real Estate: An identified parcel or tract of land, including all of the improvements, if any.

Real Property: The interests, benefits and rights inherent in the ownership of real estate.

Reasonable: 1) Having sound judgment; fair and sensible; 2) as much as is appropriate or fair; moderate. Synonyms: sensible, rational, judicious, practical, realistic.

Registered Consulting Arborist: Members of ASCA who have completed the rigorous requirements of the ASCA RCA program to achieve registered membership status.

Relevant: 1) Appropriate to what is being done or considered; 2) appropriate to the current time, period, or circumstances; of contemporary interest. Synonyms: pertinent, applicable, apposite, material, apropos, to the point, germane.

Reliability: 1) The degree to which a result can be depended upon to be accurate; 2) the quality of being trustworthy or of performing consistently well.

Replacement Cost Method: Method to appraise the monetary value of trees considered replaceable with nursery stock. Based on the cost of replacement with the same or a comparable species of the same size and in the same place, subject to depreciation for various factors.

Resistant Varieties: Plant selections that are tolerant of or less susceptible to pests or other common disorders.

Right-of-Way: See easement.

Risk: The combination of likelihood of an event and the severity of the potential consequences. In the context of trees, risk is the likelihood of a conflict or tree failure occurring and affecting a target and the severity of the associated consequences: personal injury, property damage, or disruption of activities.

Risk Assessment: The process of identification, analysis, evaluation and making recommendation to avoid loss or harm. (See ISO 31000)

Risk Management: The application of policies, procedures and practices used in risk assessment. (See ISO 30000)

Root: Plant organ that serves as anchorage and is the main water/nutrient absorbing structure in trees. Also serves as storage for carbohydrates.

Root Collar: See Buttress.

Runoff: Precipitation that fails to be absorbed by the ground, where it pools and flows over the surface of the earth and accumulates in storm water infrastructure. Is the primary cause of flooding and erosion.

Sand: Soil particles with a size between 0.06mm and 2.0mm in diameter. (Contrast with silt and clay).

Scaffold Branches: Permanent or structural branches that form the scaffold architecture or structure of a tree. The first order of branches from the trunk.

Silt: Soil particles with a grain size between 0.004mm and 0.062 mm (coarser than clay particles but finer than sand). (Contrast with sand and clay)

Site Analysis: 1) Identification and evaluation of the characteristics, conditions, limitations and climate of a place where installation of trees and landscaping plants are anticipated; 2) identification and evaluation of trees where construction will be performed for developing tree preservation techniques and specifications.

Soil: Surface layers of sand, silt and clay that also contain organic compounds (the decaying remains of dead organisms) that support plant life.

Soil Compaction: Compression of the soil, often as a result of vehicle, heavy-equipment, traffic, that breaks down soil aggregates and reduces soil volume and pore space, especially macropore space.

Soil Structure: The arrangement of soil components of sand, silt, clay and organic material into aggregate. It is the characteristic of soil that is most closely represented in bulk density measurements.

Soil Texture: The relative coarseness or fineness due the percentage content of clay, sand and silt constituents of soils.

Sounding: Process of striking a tree with a mallet or other appropriate tool and listening for tones that indicate dead bark, a layer of wood outside a cavity, or solid wood.

Species: 1) Taxonomic group of organisms composed of individuals of the same genus that can reproduce among themselves and have similar offspring; 2) specific epithet.

Source: The plant part origination point that is responsible for the transmission of benefits.

Specialty Appraisal Practice: The professional activity of appraisal that requires specialized knowledge, skill, training, education, expertise and experience, usually as a subset of a broader appraisal field. Professional Amenity Plant Appraisal is a form of specialty appraisal practice.

Specifications: Detailed plans, requirements and statements of procedures and/or standards used to define and guide work.

Spring: 1) Three-month period of the year beginning on the vernal equinox (~March 20th); 2) the annual period of rebirth and renewal of plants and wildlife; 3) a place where water seeps from underground, commonly near streams or basins.

Standard: An established or widely recognized authority of acceptable performance.

Standard of Care: Degree of care that a reasonable person should exercise in performing duty of care; a measurement used to assess whether an individual or organization acted in a reasonable manner.

Stress: In plant health care, a factor that negatively affects the health of a plant; a factor, limiting to plant growth, that stimulates a plant response.

Structural Defect: A feature, condition, or deformity of a tree that indicates a weakness in structural integrity or instability that increases the likelihood of failure.

Susceptibility: Predisposition for disease or attack by insects. Also, a predisposition for injury from exposure to a biotic or abiotic factor.

Symbiotic: Two or more types of organisms living together mutually for the benefit of at least one type.

Target: People, property, or activities that could be injured, damaged, or disrupted by a tree failure.

Tissue: Group of cells with similar structure that have a special function.

Transplanting: Transport and installation of a new tree or plant to its designed placement.

Tomography: Graphic imagery of the inner structural density of solid objects produced by sophisticated analysis of detected energy signal inputs.

Transpirational Cooling: The effect of water loss through the stomata of leaves that cools the environment.

Tree: Woody perennial usually having one dominant trunk and a mature height greater than sixteen feet.

Tree Value: Appraised monetary opinion of value placed on a tree by a professional plant appraiser, a tree appraisal.

Trunk: Main stem of a tree. Often measured at standard height in plant appraisal.

Trunk Formula Method: Method to appraise the monetary value of trees considered too large to be replaced with commonly available nursery stock. Based on developing a representative unit cost of the trunk area of the largest commonly available replacement of the same or a comparable species, subject to depreciation.

Twig: Smallest plant support structures that are attached to leaves or exhibit buds. Subordinate to small branches and small limbs.

USDA Hardiness: The standard by which plant selection can be determined most likely to thrive at a location. The USDA hardiness map is based on the average annual minimum winter temperature, divided into 10-degree F zones. Also called cold hardiness map.

Uniform Standards of Professional Appraisal Practice: The recognized standards of practice for appraisers for promoting and preserving the public trust in appraisal practice, including the professional standards of ethics and competency for appraisers. Recognized throughout the United States of America as the accepted standards in REA. While not all appraisals are required to conform these standards, conformance is required in most all government-backed mortgage loans and some other financial instruments.

Utility: 1) An entity operating on governmental authority that provides services for communications, electricity, flood control, gas, steam, sewage collection, transportation, water distribution and others; 2) any equipment or other facility of a utility; 3) the use or usefulness of a desirable thing that is the basis of worth in an appraisal of any property. In PA, it is the use or usefulness of trees and plants and ancillary elements of landscaping and wildlife areas.

Vegetation Management: The management of plants in which incompatible plants are identified, mitigation strategies and goals are weighed, and action plans are executed.

Vigor: Overall health. Capacity to grow and resist stress.

Vitality: The capacity to grow and reproduce unencumbered throughout the life cycle of an organism.

Wildlife: Undomesticated animals and their natural habitats that are enjoyed for recreation, sport and aesthetics.

Wood: The main structural substance of trees and other higher plants.

Bibliography

Abeyta, D. (1995). *Guide To Report Writing for Consultng Arborists.* Savoy, IL, USA: International Society of Arboriculture.

Alexander, R. (2009). *The Essential Garden Design Workbook, Second Ed.* Portland, OR: Timber Press, Inc.

American Association of State Highway and Transportation Officials. (2006). *Roadside Design Guide.* Washington, DC, USA: AASHTO.

American Nursery & Landscape Association. (2004). ANSI Z60.1. *American Standard for Nursery Stock.* Washington, DC: American Nursery & Landscape Association.

American Society of Consulting Arborists. (2004). *A Consultant's Gudie To Writing Effective Reports.* (C.A. Keefer, Ed.) Rockville, MD, USA: American Society of Consulting Arborists.

American Society of Consulting Arborists. (2011, May 1). ASCA SPP. *ASCA Standards of Professional Practice.* Rockville, MD, USA: American Society of Consulting Arborists.

Angelucci, K. (2008). *Secrets of Tennessee Gardening.* Morley, MO: Acclaim Press, Inc.

Appleton, B.E. (2015). *Screening.* Petersberg, VA: Virginia Polytechnic Institute, et al.

Appraisal Institute. (2010). *The Dictionary of Real Estate Appraisal, Fifth Edition.* Chicago, IL: Appraisal Institute.

Appraisal Standards Board. (2015). *Uniform Standards of Appraisal Practice.* Annapolis Junction, MD: The Appraisal Foundation.

ASCA. (2004). *A Consultant's Guide to Writing Effective Reports.* Rockville, MD: ASCA.

ASCA. (1995). *Guide to Report Writing for Consulting Arborists.* Savoy, IL: ISA.

Bales, S. (2004). *Down to Earth Gardener: Let Mother Nature Guide You to Success in Your Garden.* Emmaus, PA: Rodale Press, Inc.

Bales, S.F. (1991). *American Gardenign Series: Annuals.* New York, NY: Prentice Hall Gardening.

Beck, T. (2013). *Principles of Ecological Landscape Design.* Washington DC: Island Press.

Bender, S.A. (2002). *Passalong Plants.* Chapel Hill, NC: University of North Carolina Press.

Bender, S.R. (1992). *Taylor's Guide to Gardening in the South.* New York, NY: Houghton Mifflin Company.

Bender, S. (2004). *The Southern Living Garden Book.* Birmingham, AL: Oxmoor House, Inc.

Bentrup, G. (2010). *Using Trees and Shrubs to Reduce Noise.* Nebraska City, NE: National Arbor Day Foundation.

Berger, R.I. (2005). *Integrated Roadside Vegetation Management: National Cooperative Highway Research Program Synthesis 341.* Washington, DC: Transportation Research Board.

Blackstone, Sir William (1769). *Commentaries on the Laws of England,* Book II, Chapter 1. Bankcroft-Whitney Company, San Francisco, CA.-on property in general.

Bloch, L. (2007). *Tree Law Cases in the USA, Second Edition.* Potomac, MD: Bloch Consulting Group.

Booth, N.K. (2012). *Residential Landscape Archetecture: Design for the Private Residence, 6th Ed.* Upper Saddle River, NJ: Prentice Hall, Inc.

Bost, T.A. (2005). *The Carolina Gardene's Guide.* Franklin, TN: Cool Springs Press.

Brenzel, K. (1997). *Sunset National Garden Book.* Menlo Park, CA: Sunset Books, Inc.

Chandler, P.A. (1987). *Taylor's Guide to Trees.* Boston, MA: Houghton Mifflin Company.

Chaplin, L.T. (1994). *The Southern Gardener's Book of Lists: The Best Plants for All Your Needs, Wants, and Whims.* Lanham, MD: Taylor Trade Publishing.

Chatto, B. (1998). *The Damp Garden.* London, England: Orion Books Ltd.

Chatto, B. (2002). *The Dry Garden.* London, England: Orion Books, Ltd.

Coder, K.D. (2000). *Soil Compaction & Trees: Causes, Symptoms and Effects.* Athens, GA: University of Georgia.

Coder, K.D. (Dec. 2007). *Soil Compaction Stress & Trees: Symptoms, Measures, Treatments [Pub WSFNR07-9].* Athens, GA: University of Georgia.

Coder, Kim D. (2013). "Protect Landscape Trees from Drought Injury." Warnell School of Forestry and Natural Resources, The University of Georgia. https://ugaurbanag.com/protect-landscape-trees-from-drought-injury/

Coleman, S. (2016). *Scope of Work, 2nd Ed.* Chicago, IL: Appraisal Institute.

Cornelison, P. (2006). *Landscaping Southern Gardens.* Menlo Park, CA: Sunset Publishing Corp.

Council of Tree & Landscape Appraisers. (1992). *Guide for Plant Appraisal, Eighth Ed.* Savoy, IL: International Society of Arboriculture.

Council of Tree & Landscape Appraisers. (2000). *Guide for Plant Appraisal* (9th ed.). (P. Currid, Ed.) Champaign, IL, USA: International Society of Arboriculture.

Cox, M. (2009). *Big Gardens in Small Spaces: Out-of-the-box Advice for Boxed-in Gardeners.* Portland, OR: Timber Press, Inc.

Cramer, G.L. (1991). *Agricultural Economics and Agribusiness.* New York, NY: John Wiley & Sons, Inc.

Craul, P.J. (1992). *Urban Soil in Landscape Design.* Hoboken, NJ: John Wiley and Sons, Inc.

Creasy, R. (2010). *Edible Landscaping, 2nd. Ed.* San Francisco, CA: Sierra Club Books.

Cullen, S. (1997; Revised 2000). Tree Appraisal: What is the Trunk Formula. *Arboricultural Consultant,* 30 (5): 3.

Darke, R.A. (2014). *The Living Landscape: Designing for Beauty and Biodiversity in the Home Garden.* Portland, OR: Timber Press, Inc.

Davidson, R.A. (1979). *Insect Pests, 7th Ed.* New York, NY: John Wiley & Sons.

Day, S.D., Wiseman, P.E., Dickinson, S.B., & Harris, A.J. (September 2010). Tree Root Ecology in the Urban Environment and Implications for a Sustainable Rhizosphere. *Arboriculture & Urban Forestry 36(5),* 192-204.

Detty, T. (2011). *Basic Appraisal Principles.* Westerville, OH: Hondros Learning.

Detty, T. (2007). *Basic Appriaisal Proceedures, 2nd ed.* Westerville, OH: Hondros Learning.

Dirr, M.A. (1983). *Manual of Woody Landscape Plants: Their Identification, Ornamental Characteristics, Culture, Propagation, and Uses.* Champaign, IL, USA: Stipes Publisning, LLC.

Dunster, J. (2014). *Documenting Evidence Practical Guidence for Arborists.* Victoria, BC: Dunster & Associates Environmental Consultants, Ltd.

Eddison, S. (2010). *Gardening for a Lifetime: How to Garden Wiser as You Grow Older.* Portland, OR: Timber Press, Inc.

Ekelund, F. (1998). Enumeration and Abundance of Mycophagous Protozoa In Soil, With Special Emphasis On Heterotrophic Flagellates. *Soil Biology and Biochemestry,* 30:1343-1347.

Evans, E. (2000). *Vines of the Southeast.* Retrieved from North Carolina State University, Department of Horticultural Science: www.ces.ncsu.edu/depts/hort/consumer/factsheets/index.html

Evans, J. (2012). *Environmental Concerns in Righs-of-Way Management.* Champaign, IL: International Society of Arboriculture.

Fell, D. (2011). *Vertical Gardening:Grow Up, Not Out,for More Vegetables and Flowers in Much Less Space.* Emmaus, PA: Rodale Press, Inc.

Gilman, E.F. (2008). *Horticopia Professional (Arborists Edition) Version 5.0 Build 412.* Harwood: Horticopia, Inc.

Gilman, E.F., & S., J.L. (2008). *Best Management Practices: Tree Pruning. Revised 2008.* Champaign, IL, USA: International Society of Arboriculture.

Gliman, E. (2004). *Horticopia Professional Version 4.1 Build 107.* Harwood, MD: Horticopia, Inc.

Goodey, T. (1963). *Soil and Freshwater Nematodes, Second Ed.* New York, NY: John Wiley and Sons.

Google, Inc. (2016, October 18). *Google Maps.* Retrieved from Google Maps: https://www.google.com/maps/@35.9412741,-86.8607188,1230m/data=!3m1!1e3

Gucker, C.L. (2011). *Fire Effects Information System.* Washington, DC: U.S.D.A. Forest Service.

Hale, F.A. (2012). *Commercial Insect and Mite Control for Trees, Shrubs and Flowers.* Knoxville, TN: University of Tennessee Agricultural Extension Service.

Halpin, A.M. (1996). *Gardening in the Shade.* Des Moines, IA: Better Homes and Gardens Books.

Harris, R.W. (2004). *Arboriculture: Integrated Management of Landscape Trees, Shrubs and Vines* (4th ed.). (S. Helba, Ed.) Upper Saddle River, NJ, USA: Pearson Education, Inc.

Hastings, D. (1999). *Month-by-month Gardening in the Sough: What to Do and When to Do It, 2nd Ed.* Atlanta, GA: Longstyreet Press.

Hayes, E. (2005). *Evaluating Tree Defects, 2nd Ed.* Rochester, MN: Safetrees, LLC.

Heriteau, J. (1990). *The National Arboretum Book of Outstanding Garden Plants: The Authoritative Gude to Selecting and Growing the Most Beautiful, Durable and Carefree Garden Plants in North America.* New York, NY: Simon & Schuster, Inc.

Horton, A. (1987). *All About Bulbs.* San Ramon, CA: Ortho Books.

Horton, A. (1989). *Creating Japanese Gardens.* San Ramon: Ortho Books.

Hutson, D.H. (1998). *Metabolic Pathways of Agrochemicals, Part 1.* Cambridge CB4 4WF, UK: The Royal Society of Chemistry.

Ingles, J. (2009). *Landscaping Principals and Practices, 7th Ed.* Independence, KY: Cengage Learning.

Interagency Land Acquisition Conference. (2016). *UNIFORM APPRAISAL STANDARDS FOR FEDERAL LAND ACQUISITIONS.* Washington, DC: The Appraisal Foundation.

Internal Revnue Service. (2017, September 8). *IRS Publication 561.* Retrieved from IRS.GOV: https://www.irs.gov/publications/p561/ar02.html

International Society of Arboriculture. (2006). ANSI Z133.1. *American National Standard for Arboricultural Operations - Safety Requirements.* Champaign, IL: International Society of Arboriculture.

International Society of Arboriculture. (2011). Benefits of Trees. *International Society of Arboriculture Publication.* Champaign, IL, USA: International Society of Arboriculture.

International Society of Arboriculture. (2009). *Environmental Concerns in Rights-of-way Management, 9th International Symposium.* Champaign, IL: International Society of Arboriculture.

International Society of Arboriculture. (2013). *Glossary of Arboricultural Terms.* Champaign, IL: International Society of Arboriculture.

International Society of Arboriculture. (2010). *ISA Board Certified Master Arborist® Code of Ethics.* Champaign, IL: International Society of Arboriculture.

International Society of Arboriculture. (2009). *The Landscape Below Ground III.* Champaign, IL: International Society of Arboriculture.

ISA. (2009). Glossary of Arboricultural Terms. In I. S. Arboriculture, *Glossary of Arboricultural Terms* (pp. 1-141). Champaign, IL: International Society of Arboriculture.

ISA. (2008). *Introduction To Arboriculture.* Champaign, IL: International Society of Arboriculture.

Johnson, W.T. (1988). *Insects That Feed On Trees and Shrubs, Second Ed.* Ithaca, NY: Cornell University Press.

Johnstone, D.G. (2010). The Measurement of Wood Decay in Landscape Trees. *Arboriculture & Urban Forestry*, 36(3): pp 121-127.

Jones v Johnson M2002-01286-COA-R3-CV (Tennessee Court of Appeals in Nashville June 4, 2003)

Kaplan, R.K. (1989). *The Experience of Nature: A Psicological Perspective.* New York, NY: Press Syndicate of the University of Cambridge.

Kemper, G. (2004). *Best Management Practices: Utility Pruning of Trees.* Champaign, IL: International Society of Arboriculture.

Knight, D.H. (2014). *Mountains and Plains: The Ecology of Wyoming Landscapes, 2nd Ed.* New Haven, CT: Yale University Press.

Lane v W.J. Curry and Sons, W2000-01580-SC-R11-CV (Supreme Court of Tennessee - Court of Appeals Western Section November 13, 2002.

Lilly, S. (2001). *Arborists' Certification Study Guide.* Champaign, IL: International Society of Arboriculture.

Lilly, S.J. (2010). *Arborists' Certification Guide.* Savoy, IL: International Society of Arboriculture.

Ling, D.C. (2008). *Real Estate Principles: A Value Approach, 2nd Ed.* New York, NY: McGraw-Hill/Irwin.

Lloyd, J. et al. (1997). *Plant Health Care for Woody Ornamentals: A Professional's Guide to Preventing and Managing Environmental Stress and Pests.* Champaign, IL: International Society of Arboriculture.

Luley, C. (2005). *Wood Decay Fungi.* Naples, NY: Urban Forestry, LLC.

Luley, C.J. (2009). *Pest Management in the Landscape: An Introduction.* Naples, NY: Urban Forestry LLC.

MacDonald, J.L. (2004). Fill Soil Effects On Soil Aeration and Tree Growth. *Journal of Arboricultuire*, 30(1)19-27.

Macie, E. (2013, March 17). *How to Correct Soil Compaction.* Retrieved from Extension.org: http://articles.extension.org/pages/67762/how-to-correct-soil-compaction

Marschner, H. (1995). *Mineral Nutrition of Higher Plants* (Second ed.). London: Academic Press, Inc.

Matheny, N.A. (1998). *Trees and Development.* Champaign, IL: International Society of Arboriculture.

Matheny, N.P. (2014, Dec 05). ANSI A300 (Part 9) Risk Assessment Standards. San Diago, CA: ASCA.

Matheny, N.P., & Clark, J.R. (1994). *A Photographic Guide to the Evaluation of Hazard Trees in Urban Areas, 2nd Ed.* Champaign, IL: International Society of Arboriculture.

Mattheck, C.A. (1994). *The Body Language of Trees: A Handbook for Failure Analysis.* London, England: HMSO.

Mattheck, C., & Weber, K.B. (2015). *The Body Language of Trees Encyclopedia of Visual Tree Assessment.* Karlsruhe, Germany: Karlsruhe Institute of Technology-North Campus.

Mattheck, C.H. (2013). *Instructions For Use: Fractometer 1.* Wiesloch, Germany: Instrumenta Mechanik Labor System GmbH.

McCarty, L.B. (2001). *Color Atlas of Turfgrass Weeds.* Chelsae, MI: Ann Arbor Press.

McKinley, M.D. (1983). *Color With Annuals.* San Ramon, CA: Ortho Books.

Merullo, V.D., & Valentine, M.J. (1992). *Arboriculture & The Law.* Savoy, IL: International Society of Arboriculture.

Miller, B.A. (2003). *Tree Windbreaks for Farms and Homes..* West Lafayette, IN: Purdue University Department of Forestry and Natural Resources.

Miller, R.H. (2014). *Best Management Practices: Integrated Vegetation Management for Utility Rights-of-Way* (Second ed.). (W. Kocher, Ed.) Champaign, IL: International Society of Arboriculture.

Miller, R.W., R.J. Hauer and L.P. Werner (2015). *Urban Forestry Planning and Managing Urban Greenspaces* (Third ed.). Long Grove, IL: Waveland Press, Inc.

Morrison M., B.M. (2006). *Wildlife-Habitat Relationships: Concepts and Applications.* Washington, DC: Island Press.

NALP (2015, 5 13). *NALP Report.* Retrieved from Survey of Consumer Perceptions about Yards and Landscapes: https://www.landscapeprofessionals.org/images/nalpftp/nalp/media/documents/2015%20Harris%20Survey%20Report%20FINAL.pdf.

Nolon, J.R. (2017, July 18). *Historical Overview of the American Land Use System.* Retrieved from Lawweb.pace.edu: http://lawweb.pace.edu/files/landuse/Land_Use_System.pdf

North American Electric Reliability Corp. (2017). *Reliability Standards for the Bulk Electric Systems of North America.* Atlanta, GA: NERC.

Nowak, C.A., & Ballard, B.D. (2005). A Framework for Applying Integrated Vegetaion Management on Rights-ofWay. *Journal of Arboriculture*, 31(1): 28-37.

Nowak, D.J. (2014). Tree and Forest Effects on Air Quality and Human Health in the Unted States. *Environmental Pollution 193*, 119-129.

Parkman, J.P. (2003). *UT Extension PB 1652 Ornamental and Turfgrass Pest Control.* Knoxville, TN: University of Tenessee Agriculture Extension Service Entomology and Plant Pathology.

Petit, J.D. (1995). *Building Greener Neighborhoods: Trees as Part of the Plan.* Wahsington, D.C.: American Forests and Home Builder Press, National Association of Home Builders.

Pirone, P.P. (1970). *Diseases and Pests of Ornamental Plants.* New York, NY: The Ronald Press Company.

Polomski, B. (2006). *Month-by-month Gardening in Carolinas.* Franklin, TN: Cool Springs Press.

Raven, P.H., Evert, R.F., & Eichhorn, S.E. (1992). *Biology of Plants* (Fifth ed.). (E. Mastalski, Ed.) New York, New York, USA: Worth Publishers.

Reed, S. (2010). *Energy-wise Landscape Design: A New Approach for Your Home and Garden.* Gabriola Island, BC: New Society Publishers.

Reich, L. (2009). *Landscaping with Fruit.* North Adams, MA: Storey Publishing.

Reilly, A.A. (1990). *The Home Landscaper: 55 Professional Landscapes You Can Do.* Tucson, AZ: Home Planners, Inc.

Report of the Commission in United States v Lorance, 3:11-cv-0311 (US District Court of Middle Tennessee-Nashville April 23, 2013).

Samnik, J. (2017). Plant Appraisal: One Canopy Under One Valuation. *International Society of Arboriculture Annual Conference.* Washington, DC: Internal Society of Arboriculture.

Schwarze, F. (2004). *Fungal Strategies of Wood Decay in Trees.* New York, NY: Springer-Verlag.

Schwarze, F.W. (2008). *Diagnosis and Prognosis of the Development of Wood Decay in Urban Trees.* Rowville, Australia: ENSPEC Pty Ltd.

Shaw, M.E. (2012). "Split Decision: The Issue of Borderline Trees." *Arboricultural Consultant*, pp. Issue 4:26-27.

Shaw, M. (2010). *FUMC North Campus Oaks-Franklin First United Methodist Chruch General Information, Maintenance and Care.* Franklin, TN: Green Season Consulting.

Shaw, M. (2014, April 2). Raising The Bar For Tree Safety: Part One. *Arboricultural Consultant: Valume 47 Issue 2*, pp. 15-18.

Shigo, A. (2008). *A New Tree Biology.* Snohomish, WA: Shigo and Trees, Associates.

Sinclair, W.A., & Johnson, H.H. (1989). *Diseases of Trees and Shrubs.* Ithica, NY: Cornell University Press.

Smiley, E.T. (2005). *Southeastern United States Tree Species Rating Guide.* Mount Airy, NC 27030: Southern Chapter International Society of Arboriculture.

Smith, G.F. (2005). *An Introduction to Easements.* The University of Tennessee Institute of Agriculture, Agricultural Economics and Resource Development. Knoxville: The University of Tennessee.

Smith, K. (1982). *Southern Home Landscaping.* Los Angeles, CA: HP Books.

Smith, M.A. (2002). *A Guide to the Plant Health Care Management System.* Champaign, IL: International Society of Arboriculture.

Sunset Books, Inc. (1997). *Sunset National Garden Book.* Menlo Park, CA: Sunset Books, Inc.

Symonds, G.W. (1963). *The Shrub Identification Book.* New York, NY: HarperCollins Publishers, Inc.

Symonds, G.W. (1958). *The Tree Identificaiton Book.* New York, New York, USA: HarperCollins Publishers, Inc.

Tennessee Department of Agriculture, Division of Forestry. (2003). *Tennessee Champion Tree List.* Nashville, TN: Tennessee Department of Agriculture.

Tennessee Urban Forestry Council. (2016, October 21). *Historic Trees.* Retrieved from Tennessee Urban Forestry Council Landmark, Historic and Heritage Trees: http://www.tufc.com/registries.html

Tennessee Urban Forestry Council. (2014). *Trees of Tennessee.* Nashville, TN: Tennessee Urban Forestry Council.

Tennessee Wildlife Resoures Agency. (n.d.). *Tennessee Wildlife Habitat "Tree and Shrub Planting".* Retrieved April 3rd, 2015, from www.tnwildlife-habitat.org: http://www.tnwildlifehabitat.org/manage.cfm?uid=1102 2310162640697&category=habitat#recommended

The Morton Arboretum. (n.d.). *Tree Root Problems.* Retrieved January 27, 2016, from www.mortonarb.org: http://www.mortonarb.org/trees-plants/tree-and-plant-advice/horticulture-care/tree-root-problems

The Southern Chapter, International Society of Arbiriculture. (2001). *Tree Structure and Mechanics Conference Proceedings.* Champaign, IL: International Society of Arboriculture.

The Western Chapter, International Society of Arboriculture. (1998). *The Landscape Below Ground II.* Champaign, IL: International Socidety of Arboriculture.

Tortora, G.J. (1992). *Microbiology: An Introduction, 4th Ed.* Redwood City, CA: The Benjamin/Cummings Publishing Company, Inc.

Tree Care Industry Association, Inc. (2011). ANSI A300 (Part 2). *American National Standard for Tree Care Operations- Tree, Shrub, and Other Woody Plant Management - Standard Practices (Soil Management a. Modification, b. Fertilization, and c. Drainage.* Londonderry, NH: Tree Care Industry Association, Inc.

Tree Care Industry Association, Inc. (2008). ANSI A300 (Part 1). *for Tree Care Operations - Tree, Shrub, and Other Woody Plant Management-Standard Practices (Pruning).* Londonderry, NH: Tree Care Industry Association, Inc.

Tree Care Industry Association, Inc. (2012). ANSI A300 (Part 6). *Amerian National Standard for Tree Care Operations - Tree, Shrub, and Other Woody Plant Management - Standard Practices (Planting and Transplanting).* Londonderry, NH: Tree Care Industry Association, Inc.

Tree Care Industry Association, Inc. (2012). ANSI A300 (Part 7). *for Tree Care Operations - Tree, Shrub, and other Woody Plant Management Standard Practices (Integrated Vegetation Management a. Utility Rights-of-Way)*. Londonderry, NH, USA: Tree Care Industry Assocaiation, Inc.

Tree Care Industry Association, Inc. (2011). *ANSI A300 (Part 9) Tree Risk Assessment a. Tree Structure Assessment.* Londonderry, NH: Tree Care Industry Association, Inc.

U.S. Department of Agriculture, Forest Service. (1990). *Silvics of North America: 1. Conifers; 2. Hardwoods. Agriculture Handbook 654.* Washington, D.C.: USDA, Forest Service.

U.S. Forest Service Northeast Area. (2011, July 7). *Why Leaves Change Color*. Retrieved July 8, 2015, from http://www.na.fs.fed.us/: http://www.na.fs.fed.us/fhp/pubs/leaves/leaves.shtm

United States Department of Agriculture, Natural Resource Conservation Service. (2008). *Soil Quality Indicators - Bulk Density.* Washington, DC: USDA.

United States Department of Transporation Federal Highway Administration. (2008). *Vegetation Control for Safety: A Guide of Local Highway and Street Maintenance Personnell.* Washington, DC, USA: USDOT FHWA.

University of Tennessee. (2015). *Tree Owner Rights and Responsibility (SP 687).* Knoxville: University of Tennessee.

USDA Soil Conservation Service and Tennessee Agriculture Experiment Station. (1964). *Soil Survey Williamson County Tennessee.* Washington, D.C.: USDA.

USDA. (2013, December 6). *Web Soil Survey*. Retrieved November 7-30, 2015, from USDA Web Soil Survey: http://websoilsurvey.sc.egov.usda.gov/App/WebSoilSurvey.aspx

Van Veen, J.A. (1979). Conversion of Biovolume Measurments of Soil Organisms, Grown Under Various Moisture Tensions, to Biomass and Their Nutrient Content. *Applied and Environmental Microbiology*, 37:686-692.

Volchko Y., J.N. (2014). A Minimum Data Set for Evaluating the Ecological Soil Functions in Remediation Projects. *Journal Soil Sediments*, 1850:1860.

Vossen, P. (2002). *Changing pH in Soil.* Santa Rosa, CA: University of California Cooperative Extension.

Wang, X., & Bruce, A.A. (2008). Decay Detection in Red Oak Trees Using A Combination of Visual Inspection, Acoustic Testing, and Resistance Microdrilling. *Arboriculture & Urban Forestry*, 34(1) pp 1-4.

Watson, G.A. (2005). *The Landscape Below Ground (Part 1).* Champaign, IL: International Society of Arboriculture.

Watson, G. (1998). Tree Growth After Trenching and Compensatory Crown Pruning. *Journal of Arboriculture*, 24(1):47-53.

Watson, G. (1996). Tree Root System Enhancement with Paclobutrazol. *Journal of Arboriculure*, 22:211-217.

White, H. (2007). *Sunset Hillside Landscaping: A Complete Guide to Successful Gardens on Sloping Ground, 2nd Ed.* Menlo Park, CA: Sunset Publishing Corp.

Wikipedia, Inc. (2015, May 6). *Ecological Succession.* Retrieved July 15, 2015, from Wikipedia: https://en.wikipedia.org/wiki/Ecological_succession

Windham, A.S. (2002). *Diseases of Shade and Ornamental Trees.* Knoxville, TN: University of Tennessee Agricultural Extension Service.

Windham, A. (2001, 12 13). *UT Extension Publication Document SP456.p.* Retrieved August 16, 2016, from University of Tennessee Agricultural Extension Service: https://extension.tennessee.edu/publications/Documents/SP546.pdf

Wood v Wolfenbarger E2011-01953-COA-R3-CV (Tennessee Court of Appeals at Knoxville August 15, 2012)

Young, B.O. (2011). *The Naturescaping Workbook: A Step-by-step Gudie for Bringing Nature to Your Backyard.* Portland: OR: Timber Press, Inc.

APPENDICES

A-1 Field Data of Amenity Plant Appraisal Characteristics
A-2 Unit Formula Appraised Value Worksheet
A-3 Qualitative Assessment of Landscape Design
A-4 Model of Cost Depreciation of Plants

APPENDIX A-1

Field Data of Amenity Plant Appraisal Characteristics

Tree ID # ____________________ Date ____________________

Property ID ____

Appraiser ____

Plant Genus/Species: ________________________________

Species/Site Suitability Size to Available Space: ______ %

Soils and Climate

Climatic/Environmental Conditions

Temperature: ________ Precipitation/Soil Moisture: ________ Sunlight/Shade: ________

Wind Exposure: ________ Pests: ________

Soil Conditions

Soil pH: ________ Soil Nutrients ______________________________

Soil Organic Content: ________ Soil Texture: ____________ Bulk Density: ____________

Soil Biology: ____

Pollution Pesticide Tolerance ______________________________

Plant Characteristics

Leaf Persistence: Evergreen Semi-Deciduous Deciduous

Growth Habit: ______________________________

Inflorescence TOY: ______________ Color: ______________ Showiness: ______________

Leaf/Fruit/Bark: _________ Color: _________ Texture: ________ Luster/Sheen: ________

Notes: ____

Physical Deterioration

Roots: ______________

Branches/Limbs/Twigs: ______________

Trunk/Bark: ______________

Buds/Leaves/Flowers: ______________

Scaffold Branches/Bark: ______________

Functional Benefits/Environmental Services

Vegetation Control: ______________

Barrier: ______________

Wildlife Habitat: ______________

Traffic Control/Safety: ______________

Noise Attenuation: ______________

Runoff Mitigation: ______________

Cooling: ______________

Ecological Service: ______________

Light Shield: ______________

Medical Benefits: ______________

Erosion Control: ______________

Social Benefits: ______________

Wind Control: ______________

Economic Benefits: ______________

Carbon Sequestration: ______________

Landscape Use Benefits

Shade Trees

Specimen: Y N ______________

Seasonal Color: Y N ______________

Screening: Y N ______________

Buffer: Y N ______________

Framing: Y N ______________

Define Space: Y N ______________

Accent Trees

Barrier: Y N ______________

Contrast/Interest: Y N ______________

Draw Attention: Y N ______________

Transitional Layering: Y N ______________

Add Depth: Y N ______________

Define Space: Y N ______________

Seasonal Color/Evergreen: Y N __________

Shrubs

Foundation Planting: Y N ______________

Hedges: Y N ______________

Garden Pattern: Y N ______________

Specimen: Y N ______________

Seasonal Color: Y N ______________

Barrier: Y N ______________

Contrast/Interest: Y N ______________

Draw Attention: Y N ______________

Transitional Layering: Y N ______________

Add Depth: Y N ______________

Ground Covers: Y N ______________

Vines: Y N ______________

Ancillary Features: Y N ______________

Litter: Y N ______________

Excess Growth: Y N ______________

Hazard/Risk Tree: Y N ______________

Risk Assessment: Y N ______________

ROW Easement VC: Y N ______________

Boundary Tree: Y N ______________

Functional Limitation: Y N ______________

Notes:

Weigh the % of Functional and Aesthetic Benefits as they are perceived by an owner or potential owner. All benefits contribute to the whole plant. All benefits combined equal 100%. Each benefit corresponds to a specific plant part that delivers each specific benefit. Use the Model of Cost Depreciation of Plants to calculate depreciation.

APPENDIX A-2

Unit Formula Appraised Value Worksheet

Tree ID # ______________________ Date ____________________

Property ID ____

Appraiser ____

Field Observations

1. Genus ______________ Species ______________
2. Condition:
    1. Roots% _____ Trunk% _____ Scaffolds% _____ Limbs/Twigs% _____ Leaves/Buds% _____
3. Subject: Circumference _____ in/cm or Diameter _____ in/cm
4. Species/Site% ____________ Species/Placements% ____________
5. Replacement Tree Size
    Trunk (diameter/caliper) _____ Canopy Area _____ Canopy Vol _____
6. (Replacement Tree) _____ ($Unit^n_R$)
7. Replacement Tree Source ______________________________
8. Replacement Tree whole/retail Cost $______________

Construction Cost:

9a. Transport Cost $_________

9b. Installation Cost $_________

9c. Guarantee Cost $_________

9d. Total Const. Cost $_________

10. Tree Unit Cost = #9d./#6: $_________ $Unit^n$

Basic Tree Cost

11. Appraised Trunk/Canopy Area ($Unit^n$s):

(#3Cir)2 x .08 = ________ $Unit^n_S$

or

(#33Dia)2 x .785 = ________ $Unit^n_S$

or

Canopy Volume ________ $Unit^n_S$

12. Appraises Trunk Area Increase ($Units^n_{INCR}$)=

TA_A (#11) ________ $Unit^n_S$ -(#6) ______ $Unit^n_R$ = ______ $Units^n_{INCR}$

13. Basic Tree Cost = (#12) ________ $Units^n_{INCR}$ x

Tree Unit Cost (#10) $ _______ $Unit^n$ + Total Const. Cost (#9) = $ ________

Appraised Value

14. Basic Tree Cost x Depreciation% = Appraised Value $ ________

15. Rounded Appraised Value $ ________

Appendix A-3

Qualitative Assessment of Landscape Design

- Is the landscape design appropriate for the architectural style?
- Are the landscape materials appropriate for the site?
- Is any part of the landscape design obsolete in its effective uses?
- Plants /New/Well Maintained/Overgrown/Unmaintained?
- Hardscape New/Disrepair

o Walkways	o Arbors	o Lighting
o Benches	o Fences	o Irrigation
o Patios	o Gates	o Ponds
o Decks	o Archways	o Waterfalls
o Pergolas	o Sculptures/Art	o Miscellaneous Ancillary

- Do the landscape plants maximize/minimize their delivery of functional benefits?
- Does the design maximize/minimize desirable views beyond the property boundary?
- Are undesirable views effectively screened/suppressed/visually dissipated/impact diminished?
- Are landscape views from inside structures maximized/minimized?
- Does the landscape maximize/minimize curb appeal?
- Does the landscape maximize interest while maintaining unity?
- Has any of the landscaping become too thin or overcrowded?
- Has the maturity of plants created sparsity below — should the understory be planted?
- Are there any misplaced plants, groups of plants or other plants incoherently planted?
- Are ground covers and lawns adequate and appropriate?
- How well are plants selected appropriately to the space?
- What is the life expectancy of the plant material?

- Does the landscape follow the 10, 20, 30 diversity rules?
- Is the landscape well maintained?
- Does the landscape design incorporate exotic invasive species that should be managed/controlled/eradicated?
- Are plants well selected for the site conditions?
- Does the landscape exhibit any **chronic** problems?
- Are there plants that should be removed/replaced? Is the irrigation system functioning correctly?
- Is the pumping/plumbing system functional?
- Is the lighting system working properly?
- Does the landscape offer plenty of seasonal interest?
- Does the design meet the user's needs?

APPENDIX A-4

Model of Cost Depreciation of Plants

Benefits	Benefit Weight 1-100 Contriibution	Plant Part Responsible for Benefit Delivery
Benefit A	A%	AID
Benefit B	B%	BID
Benefit C	C%	CID
Benefit D	D%	DID
Benefit E	E%	EID
Benefit F	F%	FID
Benefit G	G%	GID
Benefit H	H%	HID
Benefit I	I%	IID
Benefit J	J%	JID
Benefit K	K%	KID
Benefit L	L%	LID
Benefit M	M%	MID
Benefit N	N%	NID
Benefit O	O%	OID
Benefit P	P%	PID
Benefit Q	Q%	QID
Benefit R	R%	RID
Benefit S	S%	SID
Total Depreciation	SUM Must = 100%	

- Benefits may be functional or aesthetic.
- Each benefit contributes a percentage to the whole.
- All benefits combined = 100%.
- Each benefit corresponds to plant part(s).
- The physical conditions(s) of the plant part(s) is (are) applied as a % of deterioration of the corresponding benefits.
- Deficiencies in species selection or placement that result in inefficient delivery of benefits to owner are applied as a % of depreciation of benefits.
- Species selections and/or placement that require extra maintenance may constitute a special deficiency and depreciation when warranted.
- The sum of depreciated benefits are equal to Total Depreciation.
- Physical Deterioration of >55% may not be capable of delivering sufficient benefits for calculation and may be entered as 0% PD.
- Trees incapable of living beyond 50 years should also be depreciated for their remaining useful life.
- In addition to these calculations of depreciation, there may be other deficiency remediation costs to consider or apply.

Physical Deterioration 0% to 100%	Placement/Species in Use Obsolesence 0% to 100%	Depreciation Calculation
APD%	APSUO%	A% x APD% x APSUO
BPD%	BPSUO%	B% x BPD% x BPSUO
CPD%	CPSUO%	C% x CPD% xCPSUO
DPD%	DPSUO%	D% x DPD% x DPSUO
EPD%	EPSUO%	E% x EPD% x EPSUO
FPD%	FPSUO%	F% x FPD% x FPSUO
GPD%	GPSUO%	G% x GPD% x GPSUO
HPD%	HPSUO%	H% x HPD% x HPSUO
IPD%	IPSUO%	I% x IPD% x IPSUO
JPD%	JPSUO%	J% x JPD% x JPSUO
KPD%	KPSUO%	K% x KPD% x KPSUO
LPD%	LPSUO%	L% x LPD% x LPSUO
MPD%	MPSUO%	M% x MPD% x MPSUO
NPD%	NPSUO%	N% x NPD% x NPSUO
OPD%	OPSUO%	O% x OPD% x OPSUO
PPD%	PPSUO%	P% x PPD% x PPSUO
QPD%	QPSUO%	Q% x QPD% x QPSUO
RPD%	RPSUO%	R% x RPD% x RPSUO
SPD%	SPSUO%	S% x SPD% x SPSUO
		SUM of %s = % Total Depreciation

Basic Tree Costs are calculated the same as in GPA9.

Basic Tree Costs include:

Wholesale	Appraised Trunk Area
Retail Markup	Appraised Trunk Increase
Transport	Basic Tree Cost
Installation Cost	Depreciation
Guarantee	Remediation
Installed Tree Cost	Appraised Value
Unit Tree Cost	Rounded Appraised Value

About the Author

In the late 1970's and early 1980's, Marty Shaw grew up in the sleepy little Appalachian town of Bristol, TN, a small city that rests on the boundary between the two states of Tennessee and Virginia. Upon graduation from Bristol Tennessee High School, Marty enlisted in the United States Navy where he served as ships baker aboard the USS *Shark* (a fast attack submarine) for 4 years. When his enlistment came to an end he took a job selling lawn care service to residential owners in Milwaukee, WI, and later, moved to Knoxville, TN where he worked as general manager of a landscape contracting company while attending the University of Tennessee for Ornamental Horticulture and Landscape Design.

Eventually, Marty took over as president of a wholesale tree care supply business and built the company from $70,000 in sales to over $1.2 million in just seven years. During that time, he married his wife Kristin and they had two children together. With encouragement from Kristin he also developed an interest in arboricultural consulting, and on May 11, 1999 he became the first American Society of Consulting Arborist (ASCA) member in Middle Tennessee. From 1998 to 2003, Marty also served on the Tennessee Urban Forestry Council. He has since consulted with private land owners, insurance companies, attorneys, tree companies, cooperative extension service agents, country clubs, state urban forestry organizations, universities, and colleges. He has worked on some of the most challenging, difficult and highest profile cases across the United States.

Marty Shaw is a Registered Consulting Arborist, a Board Certified Master Arborist and one of only a handful of arborists worldwide who consult full-time. Marty is a UAS pilot, a real estate appraiser instructor, a real estate broker instructor, and he brings a broad range of skills from a variety of scientific and professional disciplines. An autodidact, Marty brings a unique perspective and a talent for learning to any project. He has developed authoritative expertise to create a greater understanding in tree related matter.

Since 2005, Marty and his wife Kristin have raised their two children, Caroline and Meredith, in Franklin, TN.

INDEX

B

C

D

E

F

G

M

N

O

P

Q

R

S

U

V

W

Y